F

L

O

R

I

D

`

♦   A

S

T

L

I

U

Q

Florida

University Press of Florida
Gainesville
Tallahassee
Tampa
Boca Raton
Pensacola
Orlando
Miami
Jacksonville

♦

Quilts

Charlotte Allen Williams

Library of Congress
Cataloging-in-Publication Data

Williams, Charolotte, 1929–
Florida quilts /
Charlotte Williams.
p.   cm.
Includes bibliographical
references (p.   ) and index.
ISBN 0-8130-1163-9. —
ISBN 0-8130-1164-7 (pbk.)
1. Quilts—Florida.
2. Quiltmakers—Florida—
Biography. I. Title.
NK9112.W55 1992
746.9′7′09759—
dc20   92-12531

The University Press of Florida is
the scholarly publishing agency
for the State University System
of Florida, comprised of Florida A
& M University, Florida Atlantic
University, Florida International
University, Florida State Uni-
versity, University of Central
Florida, University of Florida,
University of North Florida,
University of South Florida, and
University of West Florida.

University Press of Florida
15 Northwest 15th Street
Gainesville, FL 32611

Contents

PLATE 1. *State Banner based on Great Seal of the State of Florida. Made by Grace Anderson and Susan Osteryoung, members of Quilters Unlimited of Tallahassee, Florida, for the 1986 Great American Quilt Festival. Dimensions, 36" × 60"; pieced, appliquéd, and embellished by hand.*

Preface

◆ ◆

THIS BOOK REPRESENTS the achievement of one of the main objectives of the Florida Quilt Heritage Project: to document the project and help preserve the history of our state as expressed through Florida quilts and the lives and times of the quilt makers. Thus, the FQH Steering Committee decided to organize the text around the history of Florida. Each chapter covers a major historical period and includes a brief narrative outline of Florida history, comments about women's roles during those years, and stories of quilts and quilt makers. As a group, the quilt makers were not well-known citizens directly involved with major political or social events; rather, most were ordinary people who lived in a particular time and place and sometimes, incidentally, made quilts.

As I look back, I realize that the part I have played in producing this book as a permanent record of our project has been very much like making a quilt. The narrative outline of Florida's history serves as the frame, and our patchwork of quilt histories took form and shape with its support. The material for the book was gathered from generations of Florida "relatives"; some contributed yards and yards, while others had only small bits and pieces to add. Pieces of information had to be pulled from our shared "scrap bag" and added to the work at the proper time and place to become a part of the overall design. The background material about women's lives during each period of history and the threads of memory of current quilt owners served to stitch the layers of work together.

My strongest feelings upon completion of this part of the project are deep admiration for all the quilt makers who created these enduring works of love and beauty and appreciation for the army of volunteers who made the project a reality.

Charlotte Allen Williams

Florida Quilt Heritage Project Steering Committee. Left to right: Sandy Meguiar, vice chairman; Caroline Lawrason, secretary-treasurer; Alberto Meloni, Museum of Florida History representative; Carol Harrison, chairman; Mary Alice Minnick, consultant liaison; Grace Anderson, Quilters Unlimited representative; and Charlotte Williams, communications coordinator.

The Florida Quilt Heritage Project

WITH GREAT ENTHUSIASM, high hopes, and a goal to reach, a few members of Quilters Unlimited of Tallahassee set out to study the quilts and quilt makers of Florida. After three years, interesting workshops, countless meetings, and a lifetime of memories, the tangible evidence of our efforts can be seen in our 1990–91 Museum of Florida History exhibit and in this book. As chairman of the project, I want to present some idea of how the project progressed, the decisions that were made along the way, and the events that helped us achieve our goal.

For several years, Quilters Unlimited members had been holding their annual quilt shows at the Museum of Florida History. When the idea of a documentation project first took hold, it seemed natural to turn to the professionals at the museum for their help and expertise. A committee of four QU members met with Alberto Meloni, the development officer for the museum, to explore the idea. QU had budgeted $200 for the project and had received a few other donations that permitted us to get under way.

We began by requesting information from organizations in other states that had been involved in documentation projects. We received generous support and sharing of information from North Carolina, Kentucky, Michigan, Texas, Tennessee, and other state groups that sent information on their projects, copies of their documentation forms, and invaluable encouragement as we moved through the early stages.

By March 1987 our Steering Committee for the project was organized: chairman, Carol Harrison; vice chairman, Sandy Meguiar; treasurer and secretary, Caroline Lawrason; communications coordinator, Charlotte Williams; consultant liaison, Mary Alice Minnick; QU representatives, Grace Ralston and Grace Anderson; and Museum of Florida History representative, Alberto Meloni.

We chose the name Florida Quilt Heritage, selected a logo, and received a letter of support from George Firestone, then Florida secretary of state. Adele Graham, wife of the then Governor Bob Graham, agreed to become honorary chair for the project. This combination of support gave us the credibility and recognition we needed to go forward.

Our goal was to discover, document, and preserve the history of Florida as expressed through Florida quilts and the lives and times of the quilt makers. We planned to exhibit at the museum and to publish a book to document the information we collected.

We wrote to all the known quilt shops, guilds, and clubs in the state, requesting names and addresses of quilters in their areas who might be interested in such a project. We were pleased with the enthusiastic responses. During this time we selected as consultants several Floridians who were well known in the quilting field: Sadie Bell, Merri Belland, Jean Eitel, Dixie Haywood, Jane Hill, Deanna Powell, Betty Jo Shiell, and Aloyse Yorko. With their help, we were able to contact individuals across the state who agreed to serve as coordinators of geographical districts and to organize "discovery days" in their areas. These outstanding and dedicated volunteers were Virginia Clark, DeFuniak Springs; Jackie Simoneaux, Jacksonville; Marion Richardson, Satellite Beach; Jean Meadows, Sarasota; Nikki Bennett, Orlando; Keith Angel, Naples; Patty Trevarthen, Boca Raton; and Diane Harris and Amy Goodhart, Miami.

One of our early critical issues was to decide which quilts would be documented. Should we look for pre-1945 quilts? Should we concentrate on the post–World War II era? Should we consider only quilts made in Florida? We finally decided that we would register any quilts that were currently in the state of Florida. This approach made our challenge greater, but it also opened up tremendous opportunities for us to relate to Florida's past and present as well as to add to our research in future years.

To fund the project, another ongoing concern, we were fortunate to have donations ranging from a few dollars to several hundred dollars, by individuals, businesses, and quilt-related organizations. The National Quilters Association had held a show in Sanford, Florida, in 1985, and the proceeds from that event were donated to our project. Our discovery days were set up so that all expenses were handled on the local level. All workers and Steering Committee members were volunteers, thus helping to keep expenses to a minimum.

A workshop in November 1986 brought everyone connected with the project to Tallahassee. Mary Alice Minnick presented an overview of quilting history by decades, in conjunction with Pete Cowdrey, historian at the museum, who presented an outline of Florida history by decades, and each consultant was invited to make a brief presentation. Packets containing all FQH forms and procedures were distributed to the coordinators. Sandy Meguiar set up the first "model" discovery and documentation day, which was held as a part of the workshop, and it went like clockwork. In our initial effort, we documented 175 quilts from the Tallahassee area. Forms were filled out, photographs taken, information gathered, and museum identification labels sewn on by Quilters Unlimited and museum volunteers working under Sandy's direction. FQH coordinators and some fifty other participants were able to observe first-hand how we hoped future discovery days would go. After this trial run, we held forty-two more discovery and documentation days across the state and documented over 5,000 quilts, spending over 12,000 hours of volunteer effort.

As more discovery days were held, we became aware of the need for greater expertise, especially in the area of fabric dating and textile identification. Sue Ellen Meyer from Creve Coeur, Missouri, met with our coordinators and selected volunteers at Valencia Community College in Orlando. This workshop proved to be a fine educational experience and also gave us the opportunity to exchange ideas and information and to work out whatever problems we had encountered in the first six months of our research.

After each discovery day, the local chairman filled out a summary form listing among other information the most outstanding quilts seen on that particular day. These forms, along with information and photographs for each quilt registered, were sent to Tallahassee to the Steering Committee. Members of the committee examined the records for each quilt, and by June 1988 we had selected 500 quilts for further study. Our initial screening criteria included information on where the quilt was made, the family's history, the relationship of the quilt to Florida's history, its technical and artistic merit, its commemorative nature, and any exceptional examples of traditional patterns. All forms and photographs were stored in the collections area of the museum, where they are available for further research and will remain as a permanent record of Florida quilts.

Charlotte Williams agreed to organize our data and to write the text for the book. She set up procedures for making the final selections for the quilts to be included in the book. On September 8 and 9, 1988, an evaluation panel reviewed 500 slides and information that had been provided by the owners. Its members were Dixie Haywood, Julia Wernicke, Betty Jo Shiell, Aloyse Yorko, Jean Simoneaux, Irene McLaren, Betty Lu David, Marion Richardson, Carol Harrison, Sandy Meguiar, Mary Alice Minnick, and Grace Anderson. After the ratings were summarized, 175 quilts were selected which we felt best illustrated the history of the state and accurately represented the variety and quality of Florida quilt making. We then contacted each quilt owner, and most of them granted us permission to photograph their quilts and to use their family histories.

Tallahassee photographer Ray Stanyard was selected to take the color photographs of the quilts. He set up a studio area in the museum, which provided a 100″×100″ slanted board so that quilts could be laid flat and photographed without the distortion of hanging. Owners were asked to send or bring their quilts to the museum with our assurance that they would receive "white glove treatment" and would be returned to them safely. With volunteer help from Quilters Unlimited members and museum staff, we completed the photography phase in the three weeks allotted. Some owners chose to bring their quilts in person, which gave us an additional opportunity to obtain information and oral histories. Through the Florida Archives we had copies made of family photographs and other memorabilia; with permission of the owners, copies of some of these photographs were added to the Photographic Archives of the state.

During the project the museum received for its collection a number of treasured family quilts with the promise of more to come in the future. Under museum policy, any artifact accepted into the collection will be cared for under strict museum guidelines for all time. The museum very much appreciates these gifts and will fulfill the obligation to care for them to the benefit of the people of Florida.

As the project comes to a close, I realize what an extraordinary opportunity and experience it has been. We have been enriched and rewarded by the wonderful people we have met, and we have learned much from their stories and the experiences we have shared. I hope the public will agree that we fulfilled our goal of letting the quilts and quilt makers of Florida tell the history of our state.

Carol Harrison, chairman
Florida Quilt Heritage Project

Quilts in
Early America

♦   ♦   ♦

QUILT MAKING IS an ancient craft which has served through the ages to provide people with both warmth and a means of self-expression. In America, evidence indicates that during the early colonial period bedding consisted chiefly of woolen blankets, bed ruggs, and coverlets. (The word *rugg,* from the Scandanavian, always referred to a bed cover.) Quilts were rare items in early American homes, and the earliest were whole-cloth quilts. There probably was not any patchwork or piecework on bed coverings before 1750 (Garoutte, p. 19). The quilt was considered an expensive type of bedding and was found in the homes of well-to-do people, usually merchant-importers (Garoutte, p. 22).

Gradually through the decades, quilt making made the transition from being a leisure pastime of privileged women to being a necessity adopted by women of moderate and poor means. American settlers eventually developed capabilities for growing and processing wool, linen, and cotton so that homespun fabrics as well as more expensive purchased materials were available for clothing construction and quilt making. During and following the American Revolution, efforts at self-sufficiency were encouraged and this further stimulated a quilt-making tradition among American women. All fabric was precious, and each piece was recycled as long as possible. Conservation practices led to patching bed covers as well as clothing, and the quilts that resulted used pieces and patches in whatever fiber types, sizes, and colors were available (Orlofsky, pp. 11–12).

Patchwork quilting flourished from 1775 to 1875, and a wonderful variety of designs developed, inspired by events such as the admission of new states, the opening of the West, the coming of the railroad, and many political and social movements (Safford and Bishop, p. 8). Since physical and economic conditions were harsh in areas newly settled and materials continued to be scarce and expensive, most new American quilts served util-

PLATE 2. *LeMoyne Stars alternated with Lattice blocks, Flying Geese border. Made about* *1790 by Mrs. Cooper. Dimensions, 90" × 105"; cotton top; pieced by hand; quilted by hand* *in overall parallel pattern; thin cotton batting; beige homespun linen backing.*

itarian rather than decorative purposes. Those that have survived from this early period are either practical quilts made from the sturdiest materials with careful workmanship or quilts that were prized for some special reason. These special quilts often incorporated costly purchased fabrics and examples of beautiful design and expert needlework (Orlofsky, p. 37).

While existing records are insufficient to formulate a detailed or comprehensive history of quilt making in early America, increasingly after 1800 the activity spread as a necessity of day-to-day life and on occasion as a means of personal expression. Because climatic, geographical, economic, social, and ethnic circumstances varied greatly from one geographic area to another, differences in the materials, styles, and techniques used for quilt making also varied. But certain types and patterns seem to have developed simultaneously throughout early America (Orlofsky, p. 14).

Star designs and the nine-patch block were two widely used patchwork patterns in early American quilts. The LeMoyne Star pattern alternated with the Lattice block is used in one of the oldest quilts discovered during the Florida Quilt Heritage Project (Plate 2). The quilt's borders are in the Flying Geese pattern, and the backing is of beige homespun linen. Its estimated construction date is about 1790, and Jane Likon of Cocoa, Florida, is its current owner.

Another older quilt registered during the project, a cotton chintz quilt in the popular nine-patch pattern, was made in Easton, Massachusetts, in the early 1800s (Plate 3). It has corner recesses at the bottom to accommodate the posts of the beds then widely used in New England. Both the fabric and the style of this quilt reflect the type of quilt making that was common in the northeastern United States in the early nineteenth century. The quilt was brought to Florida in 1956 by Norma Cole Attardi of Hollywood, Florida, and was made by her Great-great-grandmother Gifford.

The LeMoyne Star also appears as a design element in an elegant silk quilt with the Sunburst pattern as its center (Plate 4). Wild Goose Chase blocks and borders complete the top. This quilt was made in 1826 by the ladies of the Lunnet Temple in Harvard, Massachusetts, as a wedding gift for their pastor, R. Joshua Herries. It is currently owned by Patricia Born of Pensacola, Florida.

While random patchwork was a common method throughout early America for using even the smallest pieces of fabric, a quilt made in Mercer County, Pennsylvania, about 1835 provides an example of this technique in an unusual pattern called Cross of St. Andrew (Plate 5). The larger diamonds in the pattern combine many small pieces in the crazy-patch manner, resulting in a collection of a great variety of fabrics from the quilt maker's time. This quilt was made by a member of the Shannon family and was a gift to Mildred G. Mead of Tallahassee, Florida, from her uncle, Joseph Goddard, who was married to Hazel Shannon. Mildred brought this quilt to Florida in 1957.

When quilt makers wished to fashion a quilt top in the appliqué technique—stitching designs cut from one fabric on top of another—they often used a simplified flower motif. An example of this type of work is a frontier quilt from Kentucky done in a red, green, and white Lotus Flower Variation (Plate 6). It was made in 1832, six generations ago, in the Wilson family. According to family history, its maker was Mary Boone Wilson, the wife of Samuel Wilson. Their son became the first Samuel Boone Wilson, and the quilt has been handed down in the family to the Samuel Boone Wilson in each generation. The story passed along with the quilt is that

PLATE 3. *Nine-patch. Made
in early 1800s by Mrs. Gifford.
Dimensions, 93½" × 96½";
cotton chintz top; pieced by
hand; quilted by hand; cotton
batting with seeds; beige homespun backing.*

PLATE 4. *Sunburst center with LeMoyne Stars, bordered by Wild Goose Chase blocks and strips. Made in 1826 by ladies of Lunnet Temple in Harvard,* *Massachusetts. Dimensions, 80" × 82"; silk fabric top; pieced by hand; fine hand-quilting in outline pattern; off-white cotton backing.*

PLATE 5. *Cross of St. Andrew. Made by a member of the Shan- on family from Mercer County, nnsylvania, about 1835. imensions, 103"* × *109"; multicolor cotton top; pieced by hand; fine hand-quilt- ing in parallel lines; cotton batting; cotton backing.*

PLATE 6. *Lotus Flower Varia-*
tion appliqué. Made by Mary
Boone Wilson in Kentucky in
1832. Dimensions, 94" ×
94"; homespun cotton top;
appliquéd by hand; fine hand-
quilting in square grid pattern
with squares and stripes in bor-
ders; cotton batting; unbleached
cotton backing.

Cherokee Indians who were being displaced from North Carolina to Oklahoma stopped in Kentucky, and the quilt maker learned from them how to dye the fabrics used in the quilt. The quilting lines were drawn in charcoal and are still visible in several places on the top. This quilt was brought to Florida in 1960 by Patty Harrison Wilson, the mother of the current owner, Samuel Boone Wilson IV, of Old Town, Florida.

As the nineteenth century progressed, quilt making flourished across most of settled America, reflecting the vigorous growth of the young developing nation. American pioneer women, strong, capable, and often selfless, faced the challenges and hardships of a primitive life-style as they moved with their families in each new wave of migration. They took with them across the nation their needlework arts and their knowledge of "making do" with what they had. Their quilts—some old and worn and some in progress—cradled babies in the jostling wagons, provided warmth for sleeping on the ground as they rested along the way, and then became a familiar comfort when the family settled in a new home.

Florida's Early Years (1513–1821) and the Territorial Period (1821–1845)

◆   ◆   ◆

WHEN THE SPANISH EXPLORER Juan Ponce de León reached American shores in 1513 and named the new land "La Florida," he led the way for a chain of explorers, adventurers, and missionaries who sought riches to plunder, lands to settle, and souls to convert. Following early attempts at colonization in Florida by Spain and then France, Spanish forces in 1565 established at St. Augustine the first permanent settlement in what is now the United States and extended their control across the northern portion of the peninsula. Britain gained possession of Florida in 1763 and divided it into two colonies, East Florida with its capital at St. Augustine and West Florida with its capital at Pensacola.

In 1784, as part of the settlements following the American Revolution, Spain regained the Floridas and maintained the east-west division. American settlers began to come into Florida in increasing numbers during the Second Spanish Period, and American expeditions from some of the southeastern states fought battles against Florida's Seminole Indians while they were also surveying for future settlements. One of these military operations in West Florida was led by General Andrew Jackson, and his battles with the Indians were later called the First Seminole War. Spain eventually ceded the Floridas to the United States in 1821, Jackson was appointed military governor of the territory, and Florida became the southernmost American frontier.

Most of the territory was an undeveloped wilderness with a white population of less than 5,000 settled largely in the two old cities of St. Augustine to the east and Pensacola to the west, with scattered settlers living between. The people who were to inherit the state followed the two-rut tracks south down endless stretches of forest land and swamps. The majority of these newcomers were from the Carolinas, Georgia, and Alabama, and they came carrying their family belongings in oxcarts or driving their wealth in front of them in the form of livestock. Across the northern stretch of Florida these early pioneers found well-timbered land with springs, lakes, and rivers where they built their homes and began to cultivate the fertile soil.

As a territory, Florida was divided socially and economically into three districts: East Florida, from the Atlantic to the Suwannee River; Middle Florida, between the Suwannee and the Apalachicola rivers; and West Florida, from the Apalachicola to the Perdido River. Because of the great difficulties of traveling across 400 miles of wilderness to transact governmental or commercial business, a new capital site was selected halfway between St. Augustine and Pensacola, at Tallahassee, which had been an Indian settlement with no white residents. Tallahassee was officially proclaimed the territorial capital in March 1824, and the cornerstone for the first capitol building was laid in 1826. A more appropriate building was erected in 1839; it still exists as the central section of the restored capitol adjacent to Florida's modern twenty-two-story capitol.

One of the primary concerns during Florida's territorial period was what the settlers perceived as the Indian threat. There were about 6,000 Seminoles living in Florida when it became a territory; there have never been that many since. By the end of the Second Seminole War in 1842 some Indians had migrated to the western United States, some had been captured, and others had escaped into the Everglades. In 1858, when the Third Seminole War ended, their number was reduced to about 200. During the war the Seminoles won respect for their bravery and fighting ability, and the name of Osceola, one of their most courageous leaders, still retains historical significance.

By 1840 the residents of territorial Florida were concentrating on developing the potential of their lands and gaining statehood. The most rapidly developing section of the territory was Middle Florida, where newly established cotton plantations were concentrated in the present-day counties of Jackson, Gadsden, Leon, Jefferson, Madison, and Hamilton. Tallahassee's growth continued, and throughout the territory other towns were also growing and developing. Quincy was becoming known as the tobacco-growing capital, Marianna was experiencing healthy growth on the Chipola River, and St. Marks with its river and lighthouse was filled with sailing vessels loading cotton bales. As the county seat of Jefferson County, Monticello was becoming the economic and social center for a number of plantations.

In East Florida, St. Augustine developed slowly during this period because it lacked access to the interior of the state. Duval County, with a population of almost 2,000, largely farmers, received its charter in 1832. Enough settlers had accumulated at the cow ford on the St. Johns River to form a town, which was named Jacksonville. Fernandina's growth was stimulated by the establishment there of the eastern terminus of the Florida Railroad on the eve of the Civil War, and Palatka, which had been depopulated of whites by the Indian wars, was only a small village when it incorporated in 1853 (Tebeau, p. 146).

Pensacola had been the only town on the Gulf Coast in 1821; Apalachicola, St. Joseph, Port Leon, Magnolia, Newport, and Tampa were added during the territorial period. Although Pensacola was busy with lumbering and land speculation and had an excellent harbor, its lack of river or rail contact with the interior resulted in less dramatic growth than its neighbors experienced. Apalachicola thrived on shipping cotton brought by riverboat from Alabama and Georgia (Tebeau, pp. 145, 148, 149; Douglas, pp. 141–42). On the lower Gulf Coast, Fort Brooke, established on Tampa Bay in 1842 to keep watch on the Seminole Indian reservation, led to the emergence of Tampa.

While most of the settlers migrating across the borders of the Florida territory were poor and often illiterate, some who came into Middle Florida during the 1820s and 1830s were from upper-class families in Virginia, Tennessee, and the Carolinas and came with their livestock, farming equipment, and slaves to settle as cotton planters. These planter families became the basis of the well-educated gentry who set the standards and assumed the social, political, and economic leadership of Florida during its territorial and early statehood periods.

While some plantations in Middle Florida had as many as 200 slaves, most slaveowners had far fewer. Cotton was the leading cash crop of the plantations; other important crops were corn, oats, sugarcane, sweet potatoes, and rice. Cattle, pigs, and chickens were raised to supply dairy products and meat. Slaves provided agricultural labor and performed many skilled crafts that were necessary, such as making baskets, ropes, yarn, and cloth. Women who were former slaves on Florida plantations have described spinning and dyeing thread, weaving cloth, and making their clothing (*Florida Slave Narratives,* pp. 3, 34). Most plantations operated as self-sufficient entities, supplying most of their own domestic needs. Few Florida planters actually lived the aristocratic life-style depicted in modern fiction. Many resided in modest dwellings surrounded by slave cabins, and some enjoyed the benefits of a dairy, a vegetable garden, or an orchard.

The settlers of more moderate means generally lived on small farms with all family members sharing the work load. These small-scale farmers attempted to be as self-sufficient as possible, raising food crops and animals as well as a few cash crops. They made most of what they needed for day-to-day survival. Family members, including children, shared the work on the farm, and many of these settlers lived hard lives. In terms of housing, food, and work, their living conditions were not much better than those of the slaves on some of the large plantations. These farmers were likely to live in what was called a double-pen log cabin with a passage through the middle and attached sheds. Chimneys and fireplaces of stick and clay were common, and the cabins had only heavy shutters for closing their windows.

◆   ◆   ◆

Once settlers had been in Florida long enough to build homes and establish crops, the women looked for available native materials for spinning yarn and weaving fabric for family clothing and bedding. Thus was the stage set for the beginning of quilt making in Florida. The earliest Florida-made quilt registered during the Florida Quilt Heritage Project is a green and gold on off-white variation of the Anna's Irish Tulip appliqué pattern (Plate 7). At the time it was registered, the quilt was owned by Frances Lamb Kolner of Melbourne, Florida; it was made in Jefferson County by Frances's great-grandmother, Narcissa Caroline Walker Lamb, some time before her marriage in 1845.

Narcissa was born in 1824 in Summerville, South Carolina, and came to Jefferson County in the 1830s or early 1840s with her mother, Ann Walker, her brother, David, and several other family members. When she was twenty-one Narcissa married Isaac Newton Lamb, and they moved to Madison County, where Isaac practiced law. Their eight children were educated in the public schools and received additional instruction from their father. Isaac served in the Fifth Florida Cavalry during the Civil War and was in active service near Lake City, Florida. During his absence, Narcissa was responsible for managing the family plantation and caring for the children. When the war was over, Isaac returned home, but he was in poor health for the rest of his life. He died in 1899, and Narcissa went to live with a daughter for the remainder of her years. Family tradition holds that Narcissa was a very shy person, somewhat superstitious, who refused to have a portrait or photograph made.

This quilt was passed on to Narcissa's daughter Mary Ann Lamb when she married John Phillip Howlands in 1879; to her granddaughter Louise Dixie Howland some time after she married Andrew Hampton Hines in 1921; and to their daughter Frances Louise Hines after her marriage to Samuel James Kolner in 1946. Narcissa's quilt was donated by her family to the collection of the Museum of Florida History in the summer of 1989.

PLATE 7. *Anna's Irish Tulip
Variation. Made by Narcissa
Caroline Walker Lamb in Jefferson County, Florida, before
1845. Dimensions, 81" × 83";
cotton top; appliquéd by hand;
hand-quilted in parallel pattern;
medium cotton batting; off-
white cotton backing.*

Early Statehood
(1845–1860)

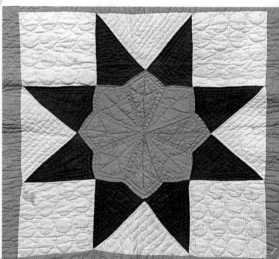

FLORIDA BECAME the twenty-seventh state in the Union in 1845. Five years later the population had increased to 87,445, including 39,000 slaves and 1,000 free blacks. Several positive factors contributed to the growth and development of the new state: strong immigration movements continued, the economic depression of the late 1830s was fading, and Indian warfare appeared to be over at last. The sole remaining obstacle was the controversy over slavery (Tebeau, p. 171). In the first ten to fifteen years of statehood there were few changes in economic, political, or social development from what had been occurring during the territorial period. Agriculture, based on products of field and forest, was still dominant. Lumbering prospered, the amount of improved farmland in the state nearly doubled, and there was strong progress in railroad construction. Florida was still largely wilderness, however, with an estimated area of nearly 38 million acres. Only about two-thirds of this land had been surveyed, and not more than a million acres had been sold by 1850 (Hanna, pp. 247–48).

It has been said that conditions of life in the antebellum South spanned greater differences than in the North or the West at the same time, from the lowest level of slavery to the highest level of aristocracy (Groves, pp. 140–41). While life in pioneer Florida was difficult for all women, the types of problems varied with a person's lot in life. The planter was dominant; his ascendancy was evident in the church, in educational institutions, in affairs of government, and throughout the whole of society. Such prestige and assumed responsibility for the lives of many others involved both the planter and his wife (Groves, p. 143).

Almost daily the planter's wife made rounds of the slaves' cabins to check on food, medicine, child care, and health needs of the work force; she supervised the manufacture of clothing for plantation use, including spinning, weaving, and sewing the garments for slaves as well as for family members; she approved the preparation of meals for the household and servants as well as for frequent visitors to the plantation; she attended to the care and education of her own children; and she enjoyed an active social life in keeping with her role as the wife of a community leader. There were no seasonal breaks in her responsibilities—she had to care continuously for the domestic and personal needs of all the people living within the plantation community (Groves, pp. 206–7).

The life of a Florida frontier woman on a single-family farm also demanded much from her in support of their nearly self-sufficient life-style. While some of the small farmers who settled in Florida owned a few slaves, most depended entirely on the labor of family members. Wives and children had regular chores necessary for clearing and cultivating the land, caring for animals, and supplying the food, shelter, and clothing needed by the family. Since there were almost no medical facilities available, childbirth was dangerous, and raising children in the isolation of early Florida's near-wilderness was a difficult and demanding challenge for these pioneer women.

Somewhere between these two extremes for white women in the antebellum South were the wives and other female relatives of the professional or middle-class families. These women lived in or near the small towns and often had domestic help while tending to the bulk of their own or their family's household needs. Life may not have been particularly easy for middle-class women, but they faced neither the managerial difficulties of the planter's wife nor the physically demanding life of the small-farm women.

Black women occupied the far end of the range of living conditions in early Florida. Although a small number of black women lived as free blacks and some might have lived on small farms working alongside a poor white master and mistress, the majority were part of the rigidly regimented slave labor system of the plantations. A minority of black women slaves worked as domestic servants in the houses of their owners, but most beyond the age of ten worked in the fields six days a week planting, plowing, and picking cotton from sunrise to sunset (Ryan, pp. 158–59). It was extremely difficult for slave women to experience a normal family life. Their homes were small cabins of one or two rooms, usually shared with a mate and children. In addition to her plantation duties, a slave woman might cultivate a garden for extra food, perform chores in and around her cabin, cook simple meals, and make clothing, soap, and candles for her family. These women bore an average of seven children, being granted perhaps a month off work for childbirth before returning to the fields (Ryan, p. 159).

As families settled into developing areas like Florida, the women found time for quilting along with their heavy burden of other work. During some periods of the 1800s quilts were produced in America in huge numbers, especially from 1825 to 1875. Quilt making sometimes became a family endeavor: the father drafted patterns or cut templates, the older women and children cut out pieces and threaded needles, and the mother sewed the fabric pieces into patchwork and quilted the layers together to complete the joint creation (Orlofsky, p. 45). The need for warm bedding and the traditional thrifty practices of early Americans contributed to the constantly expanding making of quilts. Another important component in extending the quilting tradition was the quilting bee, which provided a way for people to gather in a social setting while accomplishing meaningful work. At a quilting bee friends and neighbors worked together for a practical purpose while also exchanging family news, learning of needs in the community, and sharing fabric scraps and quilt patterns (Orlofsky, pp. 45–49).

Technological advancements of the 1800s also gave impetus to quilt making. By the 1850s greater quantities and varieties of textiles manufactured and printed in the United States became available. The sewing machine was patented in 1846, but the machines were not widely available until after 1856 when the inventor, Elias Howe, Jr., and Isaac Singer began mass production. New dyes that were bright, generally fast in washing, inexpensive, and easy to use increased the range of colors available to quilters (Orlofsky, pp. 59, 38).

◆   ◆   ◆

From about 1830 through the 1850s a color combination of red and green on white became popular across the nation for appliquéd quilts. Several outstanding examples of such quilts made in different parts of the country were registered during the Florida project. Mary Ann Wilson Slaymaker (1829–1915) made an appliqué Tulip quilt in Franklin County, Pennsylvania, in 1847, the year she married James B. Slaymaker (Plate 8). They lived in Pennsylvania until after the Civil War. When James was discharged from the Union Army they moved to Delaware, where they raised three children on their farm. Mary Ann's great-granddaughter, Ann N. Adams of Daytona Beach, inherited the quilt and brought it with her when she moved to Florida from Indiana in 1970.

A Star of Bethlehem Variation quilt that combines piecing with appliqué in a combination of red, green, and yellow on white was made in Wayne County, Indiana, in the 1840s by Mary Ann Johnson Brooks (Plate 9). The quilt has appliquéd swag and flower borders around only three sides because one of the long sides was always against the wall when the quilt was on the bed. Mary Ann was born in Wayne County and lived all

PLATE 8 (above). Tulip appliqué. Made by Mary Ann Wilson Slaymaker in Franklin
County, Pennsylvania, in 1847.
Dimensions, 79" × 80"; cotton
top; appliquéd by hand with
buttonhole stitch; very fine
hand-quilting, alternate blocks
quilted and feather design
quilted in borders; some quilting
is padded (trapunto); cotton
batting; white cotton backing.

PLATE 9 (opposite). Star of
Bethlehem Variation, two sizes.
Made in the 1840s by Mary
Ann Johnson Brooks in Indiana. Dimensions, 75" × 93";
cotton top; pieced and appliqu[é]
by hand; fine hand-quilting i[n]
crosshatch and radiating circle[s]
patterns; cotton batting with
seeds; white cotton muslin
backing.

her life there as the wife of a farmer and mother of four children. This quilt is currently owned by James G. Worl of Ft. Lauderdale, her great-grandson.

During these times it was customary for young women to make quilts in preparation for the day they would marry, and often there was one especially beautiful quilt which would be referred to as a wedding quilt. Such a quilt was made by Sarah Lucilda Kirkpatrick Christian in Kentucky sometime in the 1850s. Lucilda's wedding quilt is red, green, and yellow on white appliquéd in a variation of the Rose Tree pattern (Plate 10). It provides examples of exceptionally fine hand quilting and of the techniques of stipple quilting (close, meandering lines of stitches) and trapunto (areas stuffed with batting from the underside). Lucilda was born in Montgomery County, Kentucky, and in 1855 married William Evans Christian, a merchant, postmaster, and railway and express agent. The couple raised four children in small-town Kentucky, and Lucilda, or "Miz Cildy" as she

PLATE 10 (above). A wedding quilt, Rose Tree Variation. Made by Sarah Lucilda Kirkpatrick Christian in Kentucky in the 1850s. Dimensions, 84" × 91"; cotton top; appliquéd by hand; very fine hand-quilting with some trapunto; quilting in overall stipple; cotton batting; unbleached muslin backing.

Sarah Lucilda Kirkpatrick Christian.

PLATE 11 (opposite). Tulip Variation. Probably made by Lulu Burns in West Virginia between 1850 and 1900. Dimensions, 102" × 103¹/₂"; cotton top; appliquéd by hand; very fine hand-quilting in cross-hatch and echo patterns with feather patterns in border; thin cotton batting with seeds; white cotton backing.

was often called by store customers and servants, was known as an energetic and compassionate woman. The Christians' son Kirk moved to McIntosh, Florida, in the 1880s, and in her later years Lucilda spent winters there with him—quilting just as busily as she had done in Kentucky. Her wedding quilt now belongs to her great-granddaughter, Chris Rath of McIntosh, Florida.

A red and green appliquéd Tulip Variation quilt owned by Jane and Ron Shaeffer of Tallahassee was found in the home of Ron's mother when she died in West Virginia (Plate 11). They believe that the quilt was made

PLATE 12. *Oak Leaf appliqué.
Made by Elizabeth Young in
New York about 1850–60. Dimensions, 84" × 96"; cotton
top; appliquéd by hand; fine
hand-quilting in outline pattern; cotton batting; white
homespun linen backing.*

Elizabeth Young

by Ron's great-grandmother, Lulu Burns, between 1850 and 1900. Lulu was a farmer's wife and mother of four who was born in Charles Town, West Virginia.

Patricia Roth of Gainesville, Florida, is the owner of a red and green appliquéd Oak Leaf quilt that was made by her great-great-aunt Elizabeth Young about 1850–60 in New York (Plate 12). Elizabeth, or "Aunt Lib" as she was called by the family, was born in the 1820s and made the quilt as part of her trousseau, although she never married. She lived the latter part of her life with her brother's wife, Dealia Young, and her quilt passed from Dealia to Patricia. The quilt came into Florida in 1985.

The widely used star motif appears in the clusters of six-pointed stars of the Seven Sisters quilt made by Lucinda L. Blackwell Brown (1822–1916) in Carroll County, Georgia, in 1859 (Plate 13). The quilt top uses solid colored fabrics as background for pieced stars of printed fabric, and the backing is handloomed cotton. Lucinda married T. Flemming Brown, a farmer, and they raised five children. The family grew their own cotton for weaving and quilting, and Lucinda also used flour sack fabrics and scraps from family sewing projects. She learned to quilt at an early age and made this quilt when she was thirty-seven years old. In 1910 Lucinda gave the quilt to her granddaughter, Ruby May Brown, who brought it to Florida when she moved to Winter Haven in 1923. The quilt is currently owned by Lucinda's grandson, William Lewis Chance, of St. Augustine.

Most of the quilts made in Florida in the early years of statehood used traditional block patterns and had batting of homegrown cotton. They were made of limited combinations of solid colors, which often come from dyes made of bark or other native materials. Lucy M. Gray of Pensacola

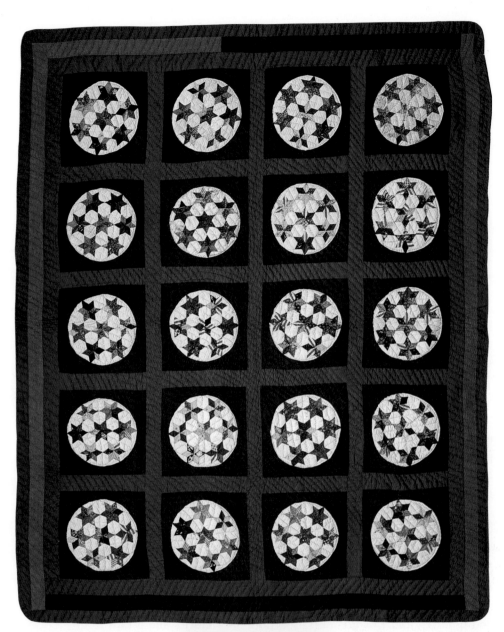

PLATE 13. *Seven Sisters. Made by Lucinda L. Blackwell in Carroll County, Georgia, in 1859. Dimensions, 72" × 90"; multicolor cotton top; pieced by hand; hand-quilted; cotton batting; backing of plaid homespun cotton.*

Lucinda L. Blackwell Brown.

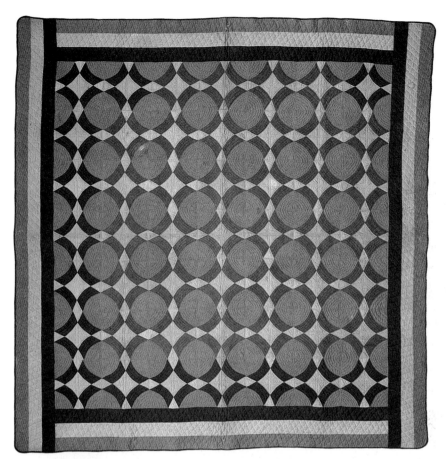

PLATE 14. *Snail Trail or Trenton Block Variation. Made by Caroline Callaway Daniel in Campbellton, Florida, about 1850. Dimensions, 86" × 86"; cotton top; pieced by hand; hand-quilted in diamond grid and echo patterns; cotton batting; cotton muslin backing.*

Caroline Callaway Daniel.

owns a two-color Trenton Block or Snail Trail Variation quilt (Plate 14) made about 1850 by her great-grandmother, Caroline Callaway Daniel (1814–99) Caroline was born in Emanual County, Georgia, the daughter of E. H. Callaway, the first pastor of the First Baptist Church of Campbellton, the earliest Southern Baptist Church in Florida. She came to Florida with her parents in 1824 and grew up near the Indians in the wilds of Jack-

son County's evergreen, pine, and oak forests. She married Josiah Daniel in 1833, and they raised nine children. After her husband died in 1853, Caroline managed their large plantation through the Civil War, until her sons were able to assume the responsibilities. At various times during her life, Caroline cared for and provided education for three different sets of orphan children in addition to her own fatherless ones.

Cassie Wright of Marianna, Florida, owns a two-color quilt done in a simple green and yellow Sunflower design, made about 1850 in Kynesville, Jackson County, Florida, by her great-grandmother, Mrs. Cogburn (Plate 15). It is the only quilt known to have been made by Mrs. Cogburn, who is remembered as a farmer's wife.

A more advanced level of beauty and workmanship can be seen in two Florida-made quilts owned by Charles and Martha Roberts of Tallahassee, Florida. They were made in Leon County, Florida, in the mid-1800s by Mariah Theius, great-grandmother of Charles. Both combine burgundy, gold, and green on a white background. The perfectly pieced Sunburst Variation quilt was made about 1850–60 (Plate 16) and the finely detailed Democratic Rose Variation appliqué quilt was made between 1850 and 1875 (Plate 17).

PLATE 15 (opposite). Sun-
flower. Made by Mrs. Cogburn
about 1850 in Kynesville, Florida. Dimensions, 85" × 89";
cotton top; pieced by hand; fine
hand-quilting in outline pattern; cotton batting; natural
cotton backing.

PLATE 16 (above). Sunburst
Variation. Made by Mariah
Theius in Leon County, Florida, between 1850 and 1860.
Dimensions, 81¾" × 84¼";
cotton top; hand-quilted in outline and hearts patterns; cotton
batting; off-white cotton
backing.

PLATE 17. *Democratic Rose Variation. Made by Mariah Theius between 1850 and 1875 in Leon County, Florida. Di-* *mensions, 88" × 89"; cotton top; appliquéd and pieced by hand; fine hand-quilting in out-line and channel patterns; cotton* *batting with seeds; natural cotton backing.*

Mariah Theius was born between 1800 and 1805 in what is now Leon County. She was an artist and painter in addition to being an expert needle-worker and learned to quilt as a young child from her mother. She married a plantation owner, and they were charter members of the Pisgah Methodist Church, still an active church more than a hundred years later. Charles Roberts's brother lives today just off Roberts Road northeast of Tallahas-see in the family plantation house, said to be the oldest wooden residence still standing in Leon County, Florida.

♦

The Civil War
(1860–1865)

♦

◆ ◆ ◆

AFTER THE CONTROVERSY over slavery and states' rights exploded, Florida was the third state to secede from the Union. When hostilities began, Florida was still sparsely settled with a population of only 140,000, half of whom were slaves. Nevertheless, it had one of the highest rates per capita of men who served in the Confederate military forces. In addition to its contribution of troops, Florida supported the South's war effort with cotton as an income crop, corn and livestock as food crops, and salt, most important at that time as the primary meat preservative.

As their men left home for the battlefield, Florida's women moved rapidly from their homemaking roles to activities directly related to the war effort: they prepared kits for men joining troops; they nursed the sick and the wounded; they opened their homes to the injured, the widowed, and the orphaned; they manufactured clothes, cartridges, and other war necessities; they made home remedies from roots and herbs to replace needed medicines; and they provided food for their families. Familiar sounds on every plantation and in almost every house were the constant hum of the spinning wheels and the clicks of the looms (Groves, pp. 212–18). Susan Bradford Eppes, a young Tallahassee woman who kept detailed journals of her daily activities, reported how half-forgotten skills were revived, relating that the older black women dragged out discarded looms and taught the others, including the whites, to weave the needed cloth. She also described how the Bradford family ran a hospital on their plantation and made bandages, blankets, socks, and salve (Eppes, p. 162). Confederate women and children from all social classes took up the hard work that their men had left. Some had to start plowing and planting at once to keep their children fed. Some became teachers in order to keep the few schools going. Soon many were working in hospitals or trying to raise money for the immediate relief of soldiers' wives and children left helpless and hungry. Many of the women joined together to work in soldiers' relief organizations and sewing societies to supply soldiers' clothing.

The life of a frontier woman on a single-family farm changed somewhat less than that of a plantation mistress. Farm women had always contributed substantially to the livelihood of their families. During the war, they worked even harder, taking over much of the heavy labor formerly handled by men. Some suffered great privations, and all were forced more than ever to subsist on what they could produce (Tebeau, p. 237).

The strategy of military forces in Florida throughout the war was that while landings of Union forces in coastal areas could not be prevented, an enemy advance on land should be met with all possible resistance, including destruction of potential supplies, railroads, and bridges. After the attack on Fort Sumter in South Carolina ignited hostilities, Confederate forces also attacked Fort Pickens in Pensacola. They were unable to take it but destroyed most of the facilities, and Pensacola's harbor was out of operation throughout the war. Many residents of Pensacola fled to southern Alabama for the duration of the hostilities to avoid the Union siege.

In East Florida most military activity took place in and around Jacksonville and St. Augustine; this area was occupied by Union forces four times. Although the Union did not make a strong effort to hold the area, life was disrupted for residents. The fourth occupation by Union troops was the beginning of the largest Civil War battle in Florida, at Olustee in Baker County, which resulted in a clear Confederate victory. In Middle Florida less than a month before the end of the war, the Battle of Natural Bridge was fought just south of Tallahassee. Union forces were defeated and prevented from entering Florida's capital city. Following General Robert E. Lee's surrender on April 9, 1865, occupation forces arrived in Tallahassee on May 10 and formally accepted the surrender of Florida's forces. The fighting was over, but the long and difficult period of Reconstruction lay ahead.

♦   ♦   ♦

With the time and efforts of southern women shifting to war-related activities, fewer quilts were produced in the Confederate states during the first half of the 1860s. Of the three quilts registered by FQH from the war years, one was made by an elderly slave-owning woman, one by family slaves for their owner to take into battle, and one by the new bride of a Confederate soldier as she prayed for his safe return.

A Lone Star quilt owned by Cleborn B. and Margie B. Dukes, Palm Bay, Florida, was made by Baugh family slaves in the Devereaux, Georgia, area about 1862–64 (Plate 18). The Lone Star pattern forms the center

PLATE 18 (above). Lone Star. Made by Baugh family slaves between 1862 and 1864 in the Devereaux, Georgia, area. Dimensions, 88" × 93"; cotton top; center star design is pieced by hand and small stars are appliquéd; hand-quilted in diamond and parallel patterns; cotton batting; natural muslin backing.

PLATE 19 (opposite). Rising Sun. Made in 1864 by Mary Ellen Miles in Alabama. Dimensions, 84" × 84"; cotton top; pieced by hand (machine stitching appears where the quilt has been reinforced over the years); hand-quilted in outline pattern; thin cotton batting; tan cotton backing.

of the quilt, and LeMoyne Stars appear in the corner blocks. It was made especially for James E. Baugh, Cleborn's great-grandfather, to take to war, and his name appears on the corner of the quilt.

Tura Ward of Ocoee, Florida, is the owner of a Rising Sun quilt made in 1864 in Alabama by her great-grandmother, Mary Ellen Miles, when she was seventy-one years old (Plate 19). It was brought into Florida in 1938. This quilt maker was born in Alabama and raised five children in a log home at Louisville, Alabama, where she owned a few slaves. She was taught to quilt by her mother when she was twelve and used designs that had been passed down in the family. Mary Ellen spun cotton grown on the family farm and wove her own fabrics for quilting. In her later years, she worked for the state making mattresses for the needy.

When Caroline Martin Lawrence made her Turkey Tracks quilt during the Civil War, working on the quilt had a very personal meaning for her (Plate 20). Her new husband, Andrew Jackson Lawrence, served in the Confederate Army, and during his absence she stitched her hopes and fears into the fabric. Caroline was born in 1840 in Hale County, Alabama,

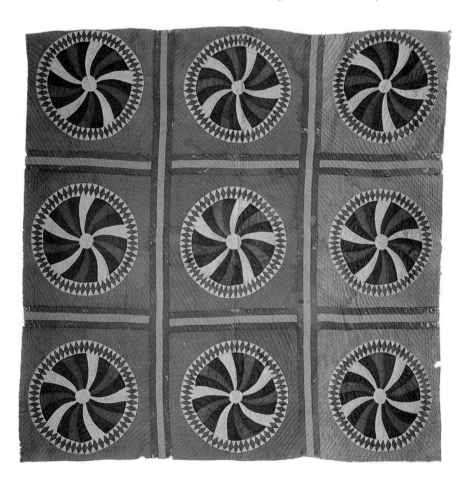

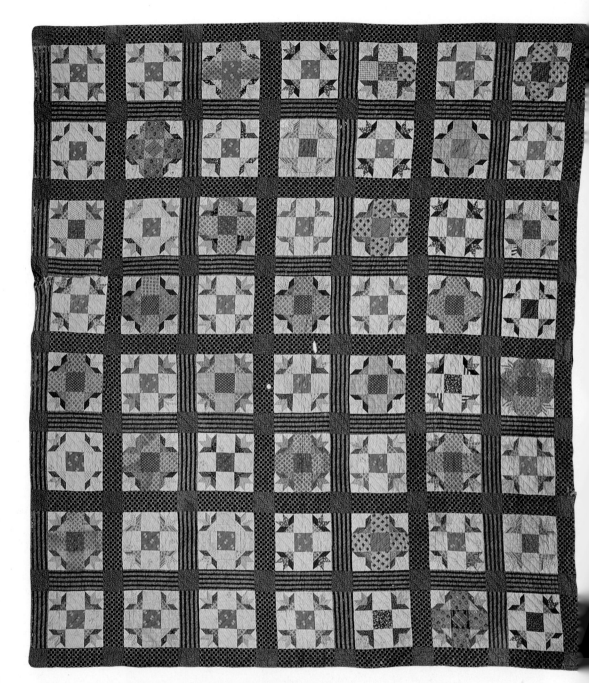

PLATE 20. *Turkey Tracks.*
Made by Caroline Martin Law-
rence in Alabama in the early
1860s. Dimensions, 77" ×
89"; cotton top; pieced by hand;
fine hand-quilting in outline
and square grid patterns; cotton
batting; brown cotton print
backing.

of Scots-Irish ancestry. She and Andrew were married in 1861, and they continued to live and work on their Alabama farm after he returned home from the war.

Caroline's mother taught her to to quilt when she was twelve. They used scraps from the making of family clothing as well as from worn clothing, and they used cotton grown on their farm as batting. Quilting was an almost daily chore in the Martin family in order to make needed bed-clothes.

Nancy Rooney, great-granddaughter of Caroline, states that this Turkey Tracks quilt was always her great-grandmother's favorite because of its deep personal meaning. Andrew did come home from the war, perhaps because of her "praying and stitching," and Caroline's daughter Letitia, granddaughter Ivey, great-granddaughter Nancy, and current proud owner, great-great-granddaughter Kathleen Rooney of Tallahassee, Florida, have "all proudly owned and been warmed, body and spirit, by her handwork!" The quilt came to Florida in the early 1960s—about a hundred years after its creation.

Caroline Martin Lawrence.

Reconstruction
through the
Spanish-American
War (1866–1900)

BEFORE THE CIVIL WAR, Florida had been well on its way to becoming just another of the South's cotton states. After the war, however, uncounted lives and destinies changed direction. Florida's Confederate military men made their long walks home, hardly able to recognize what they saw. Damage throughout the state cost more than $20 million. Jacksonville, Newport, Cedar Key, Pensacola, Palatka, New Smyrna, and part of Marianna had burned. Apalachicola and St. Joe were ghost towns. Railroads no longer existed. Bridges, saltworks, wharves, warehouses, and log cabins had been burned everywhere. Even in the cities that had not suffered occupation, they saw dilapidated houses, fallen fences, grass growing in the streets, empty stores, fields overgrown with weeds, and empty tumbledown slave quarters (Douglas, p. 197). As these men—fortunate to be alive and traveling homeward—somehow reached home and joined their tired and worn womenfolk, the sounds of chopping, plowing, and hammering were heard once again all over Florida. The slow rebuilding process was under way.

In post–Civil War Florida, as in the rest of the South, women outnumbered men, and widows were a sizable segment of the population until the end of the century. In another change, increased numbers of women had to earn incomes to support themselves and their children (Woloch, p. 224).

The 70,000 newly emancipated blacks in Florida were pleased with the idea of liberty but uncertain about how to apply it to their formerly rigidly controlled lives. Workless, foodless, shoeless, ragged, and unschooled, they choked the roads. Most of them traveled in groups, eventually streaming into towns and federal military camps (Douglas, p. 199). Eventually some returned to their old plantations and there found food and shelter—provided the former owners had managed to keep their land (Jahoda, p. 81). The Freedmen's Bureau provided rations, some medical care, and sewing schools. The U.S. Army and the Freedmen's Bureau used their influence to get black workers under labor contracts with landowners.

Eventually native white landowners and propertyless workers, white as well as black, worked out a new labor system known as "sharecropping." The property owners had no cash and land that was worthless without labor, and the freed blacks and some whites had their labor and that of their families as their only assets. Together they produced crops and shared the proceeds (Tebeau, pp. 261, 267). From emancipation onward, black married women far outnumbered white married women in the labor force. Nearly all of the black women were employed as agricultural workers or domestic servants. Many freed slaves began immediately after the war to legalize and sanctify marriages, to locate missing family members, and to establish stable family lives with two-parent households (Woloch, p. 225).

Florida was eventually readmitted to the Union in 1868 under a new constitution which gave equal rights to all men rather than only to free white men. Many southern whites still resented the restrictions imposed by the federal government and the legal equality given to blacks, and Reconstruction evolved into a series of political battles which gradually eroded the blacks' freedom.

The election of 1876 brought the end of radical Republican Reconstruction. Native white Democrats regained political power throughout the South. In Florida these leaders believed that future progress lay in new economic directions: the development of railroads, factories, and cities. Conservative southern leaders were determined to run a tight ship financially in order to encourage northern investment; they supported low taxes and honest, economical government. Their only real extravagance was the manner in which they opened up the state's natural resources to exploitation. State land was donated to the railroads and sold to northern industrialists for ridiculously low prices, and lumber interests bought up great tracts of thousands of acres of prime timberland. In the early 1870s the potential emerged for growing citrus commercially in Florida, and by 1875 many city lots as well as acres on every country road in the middle of the state were planted in orange trees.

Some progress occurred in higher education. Seminaries were established in Gainesville in 1853 for East Florida and in Tallahassee in 1856 for West Florida; the Florida Agricultural College opened at Lake City in 1870; and the State Normal School for Negroes began in Tallahassee in 1887.

The development of railroads by Henry Plant opened the state from the Tampa area to central Florida, and in 1883 phosphate was discovered in the Peace River Valley, leading to further development around that part of the state. The development of railroads and luxury tourist hotels down the

A Seminole woman assembling strips of intricate patchwork to be used in making blouses, skirts, and jackets. (By permission of Photographic Collection of State Archives, Florida Bureau of Archives and Records Management, Department of State.)

east coast by Henry Flagler spurred growth southward to Miami, which incorporated in 1896. Jacksonville was also coming back to life during these postwar years with new sawmills, warehouses, and other types of commercial building. By 1896 travelers could ride from northern cities through Jacksonville on the way down the coast to the little village of Miami.

Many of the settlers who opened up the lower east and west coast frontiers of Florida during this time led nearly primitive lives. These rugged newcomers, sometimes referred to as Florida "Crackers" (from the sound of the long whips they used to drive their cattle), faced difficult circumstances. They battled insects with smudge fires both outside and inside their log houses. Rattlesnakes, wildcats, panthers, wolves, bears, and alligators preyed on their domestic animals and sometimes threatened human lives. Some of these settlers worked at logging and sawmilling, and they drove their rickety oxcarts along wooded roads or came in barefooted to boat landings to trade skins or wild meat for bacon, calico, and tobacco (Douglas, pp. 229–31).

The Seminole Indians who had disappeared into the Everglades in the 1850s had established a way of life adapted to their natural surroundings. Groups of several generations set up camps of five or six chickees (their traditional open-sided stilt houses covered with palmetto thatching), where they raised animals and crops. They made grass and palmetto baskets and beaded jewelry, and when hand-turned sewing machines became available to them, the Seminole women made colorful and intricate patchwork. The designs of their distinctive fabric are created by machine stitching long, narrow strips of contrasting colors together lengthwise, cutting crosswise across the seams to form new strips, and reassembling the cut segments into an endless variety of geometric patterns. These patchwork fabrics are not quilted but are used unbacked to make jackets, vests, and skirts. Examples of Seminole patchwork appear in two quilts selected for this book (see pages 203, 216).

As the 1800s drew to a close, the United States was involved in a brief war that had definite effects on life in Florida—the Spanish-American War. Lasting only a few months in 1898, it resulted in Cuba's independence from Spain and U.S. acquisition of the Philippines and Guam in the Pacific and Puerto Rico in the Caribbean. During the brief conflict, military training camps were set up across the nation, including centers in Tampa and Jacksonville. Some 25,000 troops assembled in Tampa, the point of departure for American forces heading for Cuba. Tampa's business economy experienced a surge of activity, and the whole nation became more aware of Florida's beauty and desirable climate. The residual effect was the type of population explosion familiar to twentieth-century Floridians.

During and following Reconstruction, Florida's women continued to face many challenges and difficult conditions. Middle-class and small-farm women still worked long hours to provide for their families, their daily lives not drastically changed from what they had experienced before the war unless the husband or father had been injured or killed in the war. The women whose lives had revolved around the plantations adapted to new life-styles. The plantation owner and his family had to develop a new way of living—some through participating in sharecropping with freed

Women laundering quilts out-doors. Jefferson County, 1880s. (By permission of Photographic Collection of State Archives, Florida Bureau of Archives and Records Management, Department of State.)

slaves or poor white people, others moving into new occupations or professions. The other people who had been tied to plantation life, the black women and their families, were left with few resources for dealing with their needs and faced greater hardships in providing the most basic essentials for their families. Most of the freed black women worked under the sharecropping system or went into domestic work in the homes of white families. Only a few blacks were able to cling to small parcels of land, and they were gradually losing the gains the war had brought them. By the late 1800s it appeared that northerners and southerners alike were interested only in profiting from whatever economic developments the area could support (Douglas, p. 231).

♦   ♦   ♦

In homes and communities throughout the state most Florida quilt makers continued to follow the traditional patterns and techniques and to use cotton fabrics for their patchwork and appliqué. Quilt patterns or types of quilts that were popular across the country during this period included Log Cabin, New York Beauty, Irish Chain, the album block quilt, and the friendship quilt. By the later decades of the 1800s, patchwork was part of the full-blown popularity of Victorian decor, and quilts could be found in parlors as well as bedrooms. Crazy quilts became especially popular from 1875 to 1900, in keeping with the Victorian love of fancy work and all types of embellishments. The crazy quilt fad was probably influenced by the popularity of the Japanese pavilion of the Centennial Exhibition in Philadelphia in 1876. A great deal of interest was focused on the assymetrical and exotic works in silk exhibited by the Japanese (Gunn, p. 154). The makers of crazy quilts used unusual and luxurious fabric scraps in rich colors, collected from friends and relatives—pieces of wedding dresses, ribbons, men's ties, satin, velvet, moirés, and brocades. Both patches and seams were lavishly embroidered, and many of these quilts contain a great deal of family history.

The FQH Project registered a number of quilts made in other parts of the country that are examples of patterns and types popular during the fourth quarter of the nineteenth century. Florine and William Campbell of Sarasota, Florida, own a Pineapple quilt, sometimes considered a variation of the Log Cabin, made by William's great-grandmother, Florence Minter (1852–1933), between 1865 and 1900 in eastern Kentucky (Plate 21). Florence was a farmer's wife who raised nine children. Her mother taught her to quilt when she was a teenager, and they used whatever fabric was available as they quilted on a frame in the family home. The women of the family made quilts for everyday use and sometimes for church raffles, and

PLATE 21. *Pineapple. Probably made by Florence Minter between 1865 and 1900 in eastern Kentucky. Dimensions, 77″ × 84½″; top made of a variety of fabrics including wool and silk; pieced by machine; fine hand-quilting; no batting; brown backing with maroon strip added.*

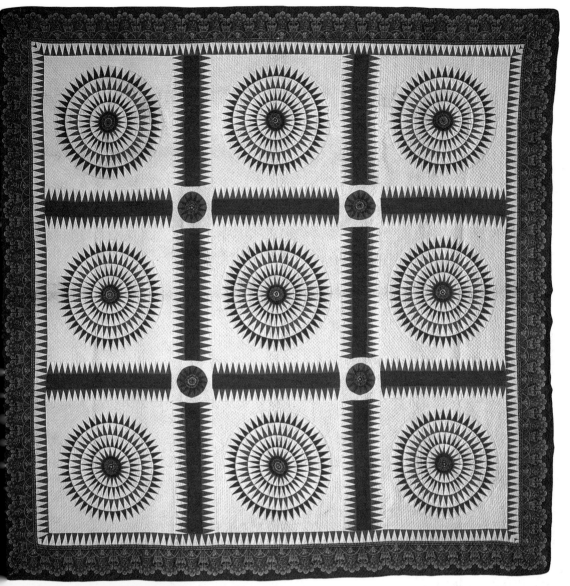

PLATE 22. *Compass Varia-
tion. Made about 1870 by Clara
Elizabeth Hart in Georgia. Dimensions, 94" × 95"; cotton
top; lacy print border around
pieced center portion; pieced by
hand; very fine hand-quilting in
crosshatch and outline by the
piece; thin cotton batting with
seeds; cotton backing.*

Clara Elizabeth Hart.

they all enjoyed quilting bees in their community. Since family records were destroyed in 1930 when their home burned, there is some possibility that the quilt was made by William's grandmother, Florence Minter Shepherd. The quilt was brought to Florida in 1954.

A meticulously pieced Compass Variation quilt made about 1870 was donated to the Museum of Florida History by Elizabeth H. Ellis of Coral Gables, Florida, at the time FQH registered the quilt (Plate 22). It was made by Clara Elizabeth Hart (1853–1934), Elizabeth's great-aunt, who was born in Leon County, Florida. The Hart family lived at the time in the Miccosukee area of the county on a plantation known as Chocolate Hill. After Elizabeth's grandfather, Buckley Fuller Hart, and his wife died, "Auntie" Clara raised Elizabeth's mother and her two sisters and a brother. Clara made the Compass quilt while she was living in Georgia. She later moved to Coronado, California, where she lived for the rest of her life. The quilt was brought to Florida in 1958.

Another popular type of quilt during this era was the friendship quilt containing embroidered signatures. Muriel Rusk of Hollywood, Florida, owns such a quilt done in the Christian Cross pattern, made in 1871 in Cherokee County, Georgia, for a distant cousin of her husband (Plate 23). A group of friends constructed it for Dr. William John Rusk, a physician who was practicing at Clarkesville, Georgia, at the time. The quilt came to Florida about 1987.

An appliquéd wedding quilt was made in Lewisburg, Pennsylvania, about 1875 by Emily M. Flick Wickwire (1860–1934), the grandmother of the quilt's current owner, Mary S. Carter of Hernando, Florida (Plate 24). Emily's quilt combines five different appliqué designs and features a border of appliquéd hearts. She was born in Lewisburg and learned to quilt from her mother when she was only six or seven years old. Quilt making became her chief hobby, and she completed this quilt as part of her hope chest. She graduated from the Young Ladies Grammar School in 1880 and married Scott F. Wickwire, owner of a knife factory, in 1882. In 1891 the family moved to Constable, Florida, in the St. Petersburg area and brought this quilt with them by horse and buggy. Emily's husband became a citrus grove owner in Florida, and the couple raised four children there. For the rest of her life she continued to make quilts in Florida.

Stylized flower designs remained popular in this period for appliquéd quilts. A beautiful example of this type is the red and green Rose Variation quilt made in the 1870s in Alledonia, Ohio, by Emeline Hayward Brown (Plate 25). It became the inspiration more than a hundred years later for a copy made by Emeline's granddaughter, Juliet Brown Blum of Sarasota, Florida (see Plate 115). In 1863, during the Civil War, Emeline's father, John Hayward, came home on leave with typhoid fever. He died from the fever

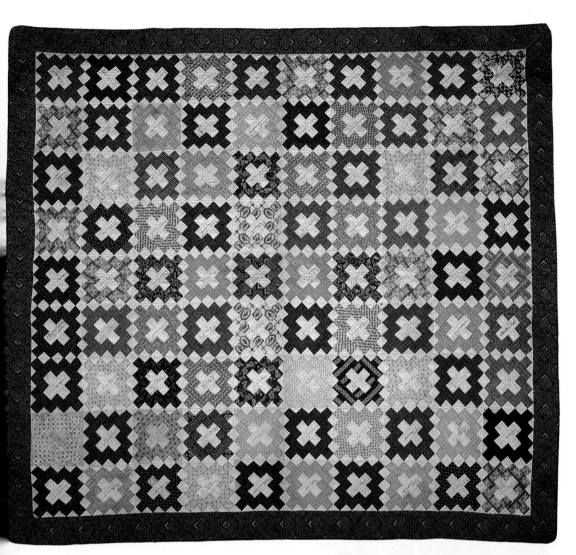

PLATE 23. *Friendship quilt in Christian Cross block. Made in 1871 by friends of Dr. William John Rusk in Clarkesville, Georgia. Dimensions, 85" × 7"; multicolor cotton top; pieced by hand; fine hand-quilting in outline patterns; border applied by machine; thin cotton batting; homespun backing.*

Detail of Plate 23.

Emily M. Flick Wickwire.

PLATE 24. *Wedding quilt.
Made by Emily M. Flick
Wickwire in Lewisburg, Pennsylvania, about 1875. Dimensions, 90" × 91"; cotton top;
appliquéd by hand; hand-
quilted in diamond and parallel
patterns; cotton batting with
seeds; natural cotton backing.*

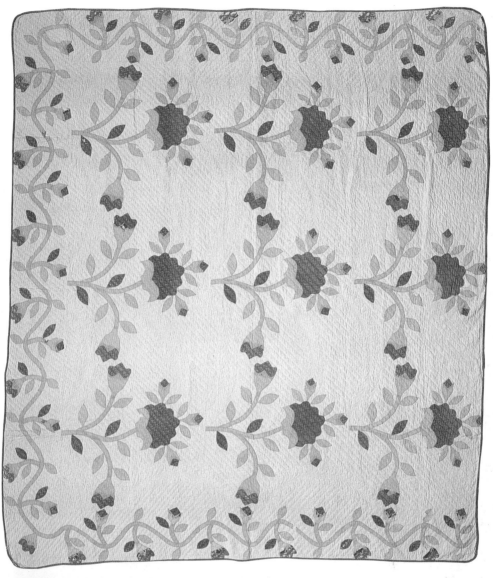

PLATE 25. *Rose Variation appliqué. Made in the 1870s by Emeline Hayward Brown in Alledonia, Ohio. Dimensions, 72" × 81"; cotton top; appliquéd by hand; fine hand-quilting in plume pattern; thin cotton batting with seeds; white cotton backing.*

Emeline Hayward Brown.

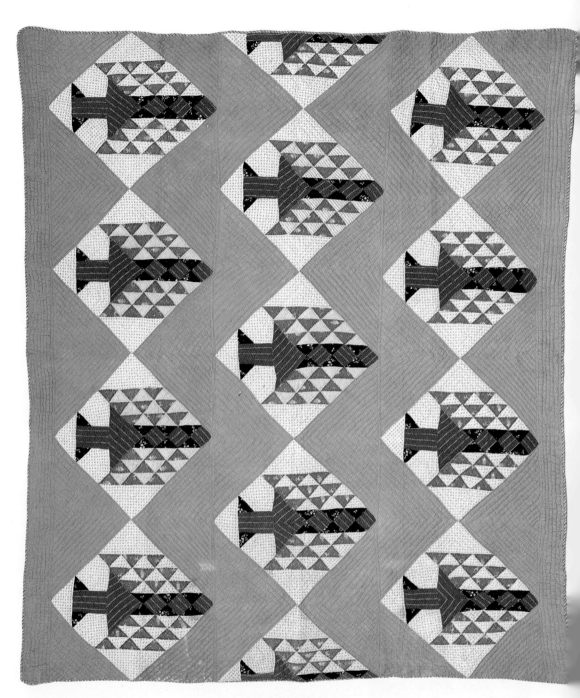

PLATE 26. *Tree of Paradise.*
Made by Janie Harris Lanford
between 1875 and 1880 in
Gwinnett County, Georgia. Di-
mensions, 68½" × 80"; cotton
top; pieced by hand; home-dyed
sashing; hand-quilted in paral-
lel and outline patterns; cotton
batting with seeds; home-woven
plaid fabric backing.

*Janie Harris Lanford and
Thomas Calvin Lanford.*

and a few months later his wife also died, leaving Emeline and her two little brothers to be raised by their Hayward grandparents. Emeline made this quilt for her hope chest when she was about eighteen years old. It is not known if this Rose Variation pattern is original or one that was shared by other quilters of that time.

Variations of pieced tree designs were used in all parts of the country. A bold example of this type, called the Tree of Paradise, was used in a block quilt made by Janie Harris Lanford between 1875 and 1880 in Gwinnett County, Georgia (Plate 26). Janie was born in 1861 in Gwinnett County and learned about quilting from her mother. In 1879 she married Thomas Calvin Lanford, a Gwinnett County farmer, and the couple raised six children. This quilt came to Florida in 1950 with its current owner, Juanita H. Stokes, of Miami Springs, Janie's great-granddaughter.

A Railroad Crossing pattern quilt made by Martha Dodson Hardin about 1875 in Arkansas is an example of a traditional geometric pattern executed with bold color contrast (Plate 27). Martha was born in 1828 in Montgomery, Alabama, and married Lorenzo D. Hardin in 1851 in Harris County, Georgia. Bonnie B. Skinner of Miami Springs, Florida, received the quilt in 1936 and brought it to Florida in 1940.

An 1875–1900 version of the popular red and green on white combination for appliquéd quilts was made in Boston, Georgia, by Cora Sibley Mardre (1859–1939). She used a striking Melon Patch variation with Cock's Comb design (Plate 28). Cora was born in Newton, Georgia, and learned to quilt as a child. Later she became a farmer's wife and raised two children. Most of her quilting was done on a frame in her home in south Georgia. The quilt was passed down to Cora's granddaughter, Dorothy C. Mings, of Sarasota, Florida.

PLATE 27. *Railroad Crossing.*
Made by Martha Dodson
Hardin about 1875. Dimen-
sions, 68" × 77"; multicolor

cotton top; pieced by hand; fine
hand-quilting in echo pattern;
thin cotton batting with seeds;
white cotton backing.

Cora Sibley Mardre.

PLATE 28. *Melon Patch Varia-tion with Cock's Comb. Made by Cora Sibley Mardre between 1875 and 1900 in Boston, Geor-gia. Dimensions, 86" × 99"; cotton top; appliquéd by hand; fine hand-quilting in outline pattern; thin cotton batting with seeds; cotton muslin backing.*

PLATE 29 (above). Rising Sun. Made by Elizabeth Guest Hall in DeKalb County, Alabama, between 1878 and 1888. Dimensions, 69" × 83"; cotton top; pieced by hand; fine hand-quilting in a compass pattern; thick cotton batting; cotton backing.

PLATE 30 (opposite). Miniature Wild Goose Chase. Made by Matilda Williams Devol, Ella Devol Sprague, and Mary Tallman in Dexter City, Ohio, in 1879. Dimensions, 69" × 70"; multicolor cotton top; pieced by hand; hand-quilted in crosshatch and parallel patterns; cotton batting; cotton muslin backing.

Another example of a traditional geometric block interpreted in bold color is the Rising Sun quilt made by Elizabeth Guest Hall (1846–1917) in DeKalb County, Alabama, between 1878 and 1888 (Plate 29). Elizabeth was born in DeKalb County, married William Hall, a farmer, and lived near the Hopewell Community in DeKalb County. This quilt was passed from mother to daughter for five generations and is one of three quilts Elizabeth made that are still in her family. Jeanne Painter Johnson of Satellite Beach, Florida, is the current owner.

Joanne E. Chance, Inverness, Florida, owns a Miniature Wild Goose Chase quilt made in Dexter City, Ohio, in 1879 (Plate 30). The quilt

John B. and Elizabeth Caroline
Hinton Fergueson.

PLATE 31 (above). Whig Rose
Variation. Made by Elizabeth
Caroline Hinton Fergueson
about 1880 in Junction City,
Oregon. Dimensions, 76" ×
100½"; cotton top; appliquéd
by hand; fine hand-quilting in
diamond grid and outline; cotton batting; white muslin
backing.

PLATE 32 (opposite). Lafayette
Orange Peel. Made by Mrs.
Coffin in 1887 in Cherryfield,
Maine. Dimensions, 77½" ×
83"; cotton top; pieced by hand;
hand-quilted in echo pattern;
cotton batting; cotton backing.

was pieced by Joanne's great-grandmother, Matilda Williams Devol, and quilted by her great-great aunt, Mary Tallman. Mother of three children, Matilda was the wife of a farmer and store owner. She learned to quilt as a young girl from her mother and other relatives and quilted on a frame suspended from the ceiling in her home. Matilda enjoyed the social aspects of quilting, and she often had church friends join her for quilting at home. She used fabrics from all sources: scraps from making family clothing, parts of worn clothes, and feedsacks. This particular quilt has been passed down to the eldest grandchild in each generation and is currently owned by Joanne E. Chance, Matilda's great-granddaughter. A note found with the quilt in 1926, written by the quilt maker's daughter, Ella Devol Sprague, indicates that there are more than 5,000 pieces in the quilt.

Fay V. Preston of Gulf Breeze, Florida, owns a Whig Rose Variation quilt (Plate 31) made in Junction City, Oregon, about 1880 by her grandmother, Elizabeth Caroline Hinton Fergueson (1850–1925). Elizabeth was born in Junction City, Oregon, the fifth child in a family of eleven children. In 1878 she married a rancher, John B. Fergueson, and they lived on a farm near Junction City, where they raised one child. She used sugar and flour sacks as well as fabric remnants from family clothing in her quilts.

She lived on the family farm until she moved into Junction City about four years before she died.

Emily Taber, Glen St. Mary, Florida, owns an unusual quilt made in the Lafayette Orange Peel piecing pattern (Plate 32), made by her great-grandmother, Mrs. Coffin (c. 1830–c. 1890), in 1887 in Cherryfield, Maine. The quilt is made of fabric from uniforms worn by Mrs. Coffin's grand-daughter, who trained in nursing at Boston Hospital. The quilt was brought to Florida in 1905.

Mrs. Coffin's daughter married into the Taber family, who founded the Glen St. Mary Nurseries Company in 1881. Their nursery stock survived the 1890s freezes, and the Tabers later became instrumental in the development of cold-hardy varieties of landscape plants and fruits, including citrus. Many varieties of plants still grown in Florida were developed at their nursery.

A Pennsylvania-made quilt owned by Mary L. Crozier of Tallahassee, Florida, is the only one constructed in the Harrison Rose pattern that was registered during the Florida Quilt Heritage Project (Plate 33). It was made by Mary Lyle Dinsmore Graham about 1888 and was presented in 1890 to John M. White and his bride, Anna E. Emery, as a wedding gift. Mary was born in 1839, married Henry Graham in 1858, and lived on a farm near Lexington, Ohio, where they raised four children. The quilt was passed down to one of John and Anna White's sons, A. D. White, and later to his daughter, the current owner. The quilt came to Florida with Mary and her family in 1974.

During the period 1866–1900, Florida's women continued to quilt as a means of providing family bedding. Most of the quilts registered during the Florida project that were constructed in Florida during these years were made in the northern portion of the state, from Pensacola to Baker County. Pieced quilts outnumbered appliquéd ones, and nearly all quilt makers in Florida continued to construct quilts entirely by hand; only one of the Florida quilts from the late 1800s included in this book was pieced by sewing machine.

The earliest Florida-made, post–Civil War quilt registered by FQH was made in the New York Beauty pattern by Sarah Asberry Brown Anderson (1853–1946) in Wakulla County (Plate 34). Sarah was born in South Carolina and came to Florida with her parents when she was a small child. The southern part of Middle Florida was a wild area of woods and river swamps when John F. and Mary A. Brown and their children arrived. They made the trip in two homemade ox-drawn wagons loaded with all they owned. After a long and arduous journey, stopping by the side of the road to camp each night, they settled at Coe Mills on land bordered by the Ochlockonee River in Liberty County.

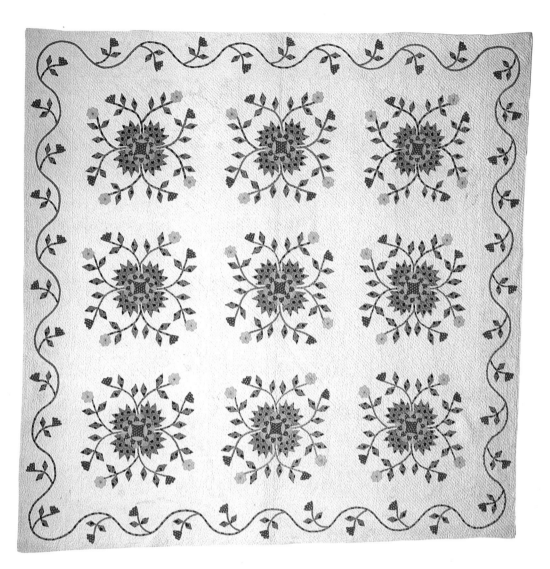

PLATE 33. *Harrison Rose.*
Made by Mary Lyle Dinsmore
Graham about 1888 in Pennsyl-
vania. Dimensions, 88¾″ ×
91″; cotton top; appliquéd by
hand; very fine hand-quilting in
parallel pattern; thin cotton bat-
ting with seeds; white cotton
backing.

Mary Lyle Dinsmore Graham.

PLATE 34. *New York Beauty.*
Made by Sarah Asberry Brown
Anderson in Wakulla County,
Florida, in 1869. Dimensions,
69½" × 79"; hand-dyed
homespun cotton top; pieced by
hand; hand-quilted in outline,
square grid, and channel pat-
terns; cotton batting; brown
print cotton backing.

Sarah Asberry Brown
Anderson.

Joe, Myra, and Sarah Asberry Brown Anderson in front of their home, about 1900.

The Browns were a self-sufficient farm family who raised almost every-thing they ate. They also raised their own cotton, carded it, spun the thread, and wove the cloth. Sarah made her New York Beauty quilt from fabric that she dyed with tree barks in a large iron wash pot in their yard. She began this quilt in 1865, when she was twelve, and completed it in 1869. Sarah had regular chores on the family's farm and the only time she had available for working on the quilt was evenings, rainy days, and holidays. Some of Sarah's older sisters lived across the river in Smith Creek, Wa-kulla County, and she carried her quilt-in-progress back and forth as she traveled by boat to visit with them or to help cook and clean when someone was sick and needed help. She completed the quilt in Smith Creek, and it was here that she met her husband, Morgan Fonvelle ("Joe") Anderson.

After their marriage the Andersons lived in a small wooden house with a shingled roof on a farm between Smith Creek and Ward. The house was comprised of one very large room with a smaller room behind it where they cooked and ate their meals. This room had split-log benches at the table and a homemade pie safe where they also kept butter and milk. The big room had beds at one end and the fireplace and living room area at the other, and there Sarah's spinning wheel had its special place. All sewing was done by hand. Sewing machines were in use at the time, but Sarah did not have one until late in her life when Joe bought one for her from a travel-ing peddler. Although she dyed her fabric for the New York Beauty quilt, she made many other quilts using remnants and scraps.

Joe had crops going all the time and kept milk cows as well as raising chickens, hogs, and beef cattle. In those days when someone killed a cow they divided it with the community. The men also caught mullet in the bay and salted it in barrels. They brought the barrels home in their wagons, and each family got a barrel of salted fish. Joe also trapped and skinned wild animals, and once a year he drove his mule and wagon into Quincy with the hides and any surplus crops to trade for flour, coffee, white sugar, spices, and salt.

Joe died when Sarah was in her forties, and she and their daughter Myra took over the farm. Myra became responsible for cooking, washing, ironing, and housekeeping, and Sarah concentrated on the outdoor chores. As Sarah's granddaughter Evelyn J. Faircloth recalls, "Granny got up of a morning, and after breakfast she hitched up whatever she was going to plow and she went to plowing." Some days as noontime neared, Sarah would take her fishing pole and some grasshoppers down to the banks of the Ochlockonee, near their house, and in a few minutes come back with five or six big river bream for lunch.

There was a logging camp not far from the Anderson farm, and the two women sold food to the lumbermen who were living there. Sarah would catch a frying chicken, clean it, and sell it to them for a dime. She sold a pound of butter for a quarter and a quart of milk for a nickel.

Sarah came to live with Evelyn in Tallahassee for her later years. Evelyn remembers her grandmother as a strong, independent woman. Her quilting was only a small part of her life, but she was always extraordinarily proud of her New York Beauty quilt and preserved it well so that it has been handed down in good condition first to Evelyn and then to its current owner, Janet Davis of Tallahassee, Sarah's great-niece.

The Tulip appliquéd quilt in Plate 35 was made in Live Oak, Florida, in 1871 by Mary Ann Burnett Gramling (1841–1906), grandmother of the quilt's current owner, Jennie Mae Nelson of Ft. Pierce, Florida. Mary Ann was born in Madison County, Florida, and spent most of her life in Live Oak as a farmer's wife and mother of two children. She was also involved in church work and had only a limited amount of time available for quilting. This quilt is made of home-dyed fabrics and includes the year it was completed, 1871, in its quilting pattern of acorns, oak leaves, flowers, and bunches of grapes.

The New York Beauty pattern was popular in the late 1800s, and Jean Morris Coody of Madison, Florida, owns another quilt made in that design (Plate 36). This quilt was made about 1875 by Jean's great-grandmother, Mary Doris Gray Martin (c. 1818–77) in Shiloh, Madison County, Florida. Mary was born in Abbeville, South Carolina, and married John R. Martin there in 1835. In 1864 they came in covered wagons with their eight children to settle in the Hamburg community of Madison County, Florida, where Mary lived for the rest of her life.

PLATE 35. *Tulips. Made by Mary Ann Burnett Gramling in 1871 in Live Oak, Florida. Dimensions, 80″ × 81″; home-dyed cotton top; appliquéd and pieced by hand; fine hand-quilting in patterns of acorns, oak leaves, flowers, and bunches of grapes; thin cotton batting; cotton muslin backing.*

Mary Doris Gray Martin.

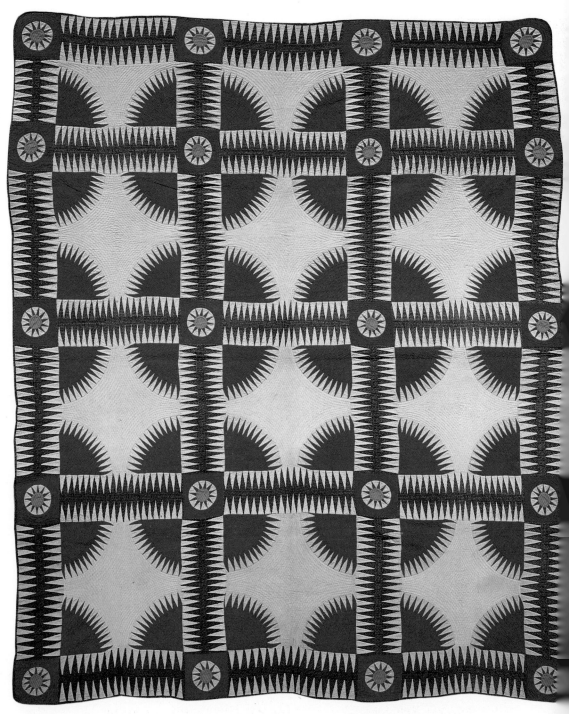

PLATE 36. *New York Beauty.*
Made by Mary Doris Gray
Martin in Shiloh, Madison
County, Florida, about 1875.
Dimensions, 84" × 100"; cot-
ton top; pieced by hand; hand-
quilted in echo and outline pat-
terns; cotton batting; off-white
cotton backing.

*Alice Johnson Kettleban and
John Kettleban.*

PLATE 37. *Turkey Tracks.
Made in 1887 in Jackson
County, Florida, by Alice Johnson Kettleban. Dimensions,
70" × 82"; cotton top; pieced
by hand; hand-quilted in clamshell pattern; cotton batting;
natural cotton backing.*

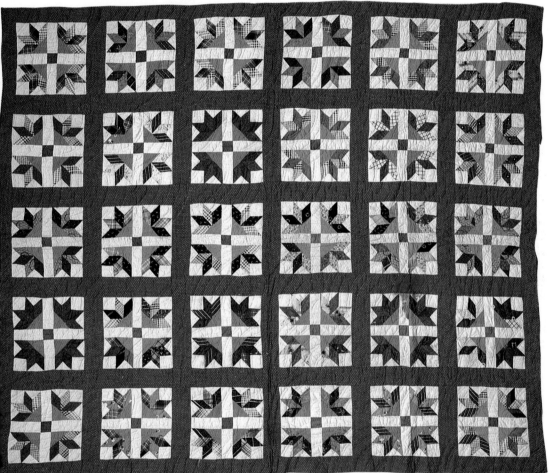

Alice Johnson Kettleban (1866–1938) made a Turkey Tracks quilt in Jackson County, Florida, in 1887 (Plate 37). Alice was born in Grand Ridge, Florida, married a Jackson County farmer, and raised seven children. Alice learned to quilt from her mother when she was about ten years old and continued throughout her adult life to quilt in whatever time she had

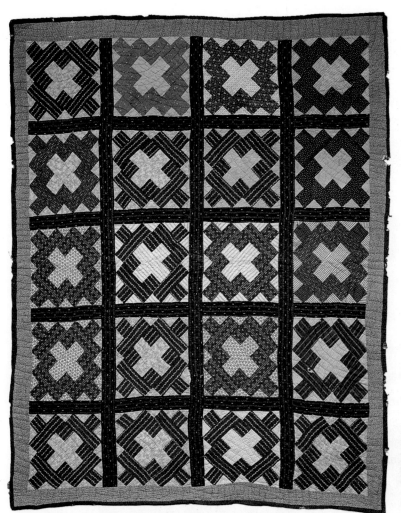

PLATE 38. *Album quilt with Christian Cross block. Made by Sarah Emily Branch Cone in Benton, Columbia County, Florida, between 1875 and 1900. Dimensions, 66" × 81¾"; cotton top; pieced by hand; hand-quilted in fan pattern; cotton batting; cotton backing.*

Sarah Emily Branch Cone.

available. The women carded their own batts, using homegrown cotton or wool from their sheep, and most of their quilting was done on a frame that was suspended from the ceiling in the family home. The quilt currently belongs to Alice's daughter, Annie Kettleban, of Marianna, Florida.

Sarah Emily Branch Cone, the mother of Fred P. Cone, governor of Florida from 1937 to 1941, made an album block quilt in Benton, Columbia County, Florida, between 1875 and 1900 (Plate 38). Sarah married William H. Cone and lived most of her life in Benton. Mary E. Finley, Macclenny, Florida, the current owner, received the quilt in the late 1940s from Mildred Cone, wife of the former governor.

Catharine Stewart of Pensacola, Florida, owns two quilts made by her mother, Mary Ellen Hudson Stewart, in Pensacola about 1880. One is in the traditional Feathered Star pattern (Plate 39); the other is a heavily embroidered crazy quilt (Plate 40). The mother's family, the Hudsons, were

PLATE 39. *Crazy quilt. Made by Mary Ellen Hudson Stewart in Pensacola, Florida, about 1880. Dimensions, 32" × 55";* *silk top; sewn by hand; heavily embroidered animals and flowers; silk backing.*

PLATE 40. *Feathered Star.*
Made by Mary Ellen Hudson
Stewart in Pensacola, Florida,
about 1890. Dimensions, 84″
× 99″; cotton top; pieced by
hand; hand-quilted in grid pat-
tern; cotton batting; cotton
backing.

Mary Ellen Hudson Stewart.

early settlers in the West Florida area, and Catharine's father ran a large mercantile store in Pensacola as well as a farm south of Gonzalez. The children all loved to go to the farm, where they spent several weeks at a time and slept under the family quilts rather than the blankets they used when they were in town. Mary Ellen did a great deal of handwork; she designed and made crocheted and knitted bedspreads and afghans in addition to quilting. The Stewarts raised several children who had been orphaned during the Civil War, and the women and girls worked together in the family sewing room. They completed quilt tops and kept them on hand until the time came for a quilting bee.

In 1892 members of the Andrew Denham family, early settlers in Jefferson County in North Florida, completed a chintz and cotton album quilt that spans four decades as well as the Atlantic Ocean (Plate 41). When Andrew Denham, of Dunbar, Scotland, died in 1833, his eight children, four sons and four daughters, decided to make a new home in America. They sailed to Baltimore, Maryland, and then traveled to Florida, arriving sometime in 1834. The Denham brothers became merchants and cotton brokers in Monticello and other nearby Gulf ports. Relatives of the Denhams in Scotland made seven of the squares and sent them to family members in Monticello in the early 1850s. The other nine squares were made in 1892 by family members and a friend, Maude Hyde, of Virginia. The appliquéd quilt squares are all signed and dated with ink or embroidery. One of the squares sent from Scotland includes printed fabric that depicts the 1851 Crystal Palace Exposition in London. In 1983 the quilt was donated to the Museum of Florida History by Esther Connoly of Monticello.

A quilt in the traditional Double Irish Chain pattern (Plate 42), owned by Jeanette A. McDonald of DeFuniak Springs, Florida, was made in Walton County, Florida, before 1895 by Sarah Catherine Broxson Anderson (1839–1911), Jeanette's grandmother. The U.S. Census records place Sarah's famiy in Walton County, Florida, in 1830, with her father, Thomas G. Broxson, listed as head of household. Sarah was born in Walton County in 1839, married farmer Angus L. Anderson in 1857, and lived in northwestern Florida all her life.

Sarah's husband fought with the Confederate forces during the Civil War, and the family history chronicles the hardships they both endured: "After three years of arduous military service, the Civil War soldier (at least those who really did the soldiering) was practically in rags. Also any clothing supplied was literally handmade—not just sewed. The cotton was planted, harvested, ginned, spun into thread, and woven into cloth— then, also by hand, sewed into garments. This was all accomplished by grandma and whatever help was left at home." When Angus was wounded,

PLATE 41. *Album quilt. Completed in Monticello, Florida, in 1892 by members of the Andrew Denham family; now a part of the collection of the Museum of Florida History, Tallahassee.*

Dimensions, 85½" × 86"; chintz top appliquéd on cotton background; hand-appliquéd; hand-quilted in fan pattern; cotton batting; cotton backing.

PLATE 42. *Double Irish Chain. Made by Sarah Catherine Broxson Anderson in Walton County, Florida, before 1895. Dimensions, 69" × 80"; cotton top; pieced by hand and sewing machine; hand-quilted; cotton batting; cotton backing.*

Sarah Catherine Broxson Anderson and Angus L. Anderson.

*John Roderick and Anna
Melinda King Anderson.*

Sarah left their home in Sandy Creek and went to St. Marks to nurse him. She remained there with him for three months until he was well enough to be up and about. This quilt was given to Sarah's grandson, John R. Anderson, and his bride, Anna King, as a wedding gift in 1895.

Jeanette A. McDonald also owns a quilt in the Shooting Star pattern, made by her mother and Sarah's daughter, Anna Melinda King Anderson (1875–1960), in Walton County, Florida, before 1895 (Plate 43). Anna was born in Walton County and lived there all her life.

Two beautiful quilts made by Elizabeth Ann Love Wilson (c. 1821–1901) in Gadsden County, Florida, about 1895 are now owned by her great-great-granddaughter, Elizabeth Fraleigh O'Toole, of Tallahassee, Florida. One of these quilts is an appliquéd Whig Rose Variation (Plate 44), the other an original design that combines the Pine Tree, Tulip, and Rose blocks (Plate 45).

Elizabeth's diary indicates that her parents came with other family members to Florida in 1823 from Telfair County, Georgia, when she was a little more than a year old. She described Florida as an Indian wilderness when the family first settled there. She married Isaac Wilson, who had come to Florida in 1845, and they lived in Monticello in Jefferson County, Florida, for four years. In the fifth year of their marriage the Wilsons moved to Gadsden County and settled on a farm in the Sycamore neighborhood, where they made their living by farming. When her husband died in 1879, Elizabeth was left with six children to raise. Both Elizabeth and Isaac are buried in the Love family cemetery, about four miles west of Quincy, Florida, on land that had been part of the family plantation.

PLATE 43. *Shooting Star.*
Made by Anna Melinda King
Anderson in Walton County,
Florida, before 1895. Dimen-
sions, 64¼" × 87¾"; cotton
top; pieced by hand; hand-
quilted; cotton batting; cotton
backing.

PLATE 44. *Whig Rose Varia-*
tion. Made by Elizabeth Ann
Love Wilson in Gadsden
County, Florida, about 1895.
Dimensions, 76½" × 96½";
cotton top; appliquéd by hand;
fine hand-quilting in echo and
crosshatch patterns; cotton bat-
ting; natural cotton backing.

PLATE 45. *Pine Tree, Tulip, and Rose. Made by Elizabeth Ann Love Wilson in Gadsden County, Florida, in 1895. Dimensions, 73½" × 73½"; cotton top; pieced and appliquéd by hand; hand-quilted in echo pattern; cotton batting; off-white cotton backing. Inscription on front: "1895. Presented by her grandmother, E. A. Wilson, Quincy, Florida."*

Isaac and Elizabeth Ann Love Wilson.

PLATE 46. *Masonic symbol appliqué. Made by Hanna Bruce Smith Davis about 1900 in northwestern Florida. Di-* *mensions, 66" × 84"; cotton top; appliquéd by hand; hand-quilted; cotton batting with seeds; white cotton backing.*

PLATE 47. *"Mary Jane,"
crazy-quilt blocks. Made in
Taylor, Baker County, Florida,
by Mary Jane Conner Bennett
in the late 1890s or early 1900s.
Dimensions, 66" × 73"; cotton
top; pieced by machine; hand-
quilted in fan pattern; cotton
batting; cotton backing.*

*Mary Jane Conner Bennett and
Jesse Bennett.*

Masonic symbols form the design motif for an unusual appliquéd quilt owned by William A. Davis of Tallahassee, Florida (Plate 46). It was made in northwest Florida by Hanna Bruce Smith Davis, the great-great-grandmother of the owner. Hanna was born about 1840 in Scotland and came to America as a small child. According to family history, her father was a sea captain who brought his wife and two young daughters to America and was later lost at sea. Hanna had eleven children, and this quilt was made for her son William Kemper Davis around 1900.

An interesting quilt made of crazy-quilted blocks was constructed by Mary Jane Conner Bennett (1872–1946) near Taylor, in Baker County, Florida, in the late 1890s or early 1900s (Plate 47). The family always called the quilt pattern "Mary Jane," and it now belongs to Lettie V. Thomas of Macclenny, Florida, the granddaughter of its maker.

Mary Jane was born in 1872 and, following her mother's instructions, learned to quilt when she was twelve. She married Jesse Bennett, a cotton grower, and lived on a farm at Connersville, Florida (also in Baker County), the rest of her life. Mary Jane's home, family, and farm took up most of her time, since they had ten children and she also helped her husband with the farming. They grew cotton, sugarcane, and peanuts as cash crops in addition to the vegetables, hogs, and cows raised for family consumption. The cotton used as the batting in this quilt was grown on the farm and Mary Jane and Jesse hand-carded it, although she purchased most of the fabric that she used in her quilting. Mary Jane created her own quilt designs, built her own quilting frames, and could turn out a quilt in two weeks. She made quilts for her own family, other relatives, and friends. When Mary Jane died, the quilt was passed on to her daughter and later to her granddaughter.

The Early
Twentieth Century
through World
War I (1900–1919)

♦   ♦   ♦

AS THE NEW CENTURY dawned, Florida seemed to be blessed with boun-
teous natural resources and endless opportunities. The state experienced
continued population growth, reaching about half a million by 1900. Jacksonville was the largest city in Florida with about 28,000 people, while
Pensacola had approximately 18,000 and Key West about 17,000.

Across the nation there was a reaction to the strong influence of big
business in America, and the Progressive Era was the result. This populist
movement called for nationalization of railroads and banks and a graduated income tax. When William Sherman Jennings became Florida's governor in 1901 with an antirailroad, anticorporation agenda, millions of
acres of state-owned land had already been ceded to the railroads. As a
result of Jennings's efforts, however, the state did retain ownership of most
of the Everglades. The next governor, Napoleon Bonaparte Broward, continued the effort to save remaining public lands for the state and was also
determined to drain the Everglades, although he was unsuccessful. Under
Broward, education received a major boost when the legislature passed the
Buckman Act to consolidate the state's educational institutions into four
schools: an institution for white males in Gainesville, the University of
Florida; another for white females in Tallahassee, the Florida State College for Women (now Florida State University); a vocationally oriented
school for blacks in Tallahassee, the Florida Agricultural and Mechanical
College; and a school for deaf and blind students in St. Augustine, the
Insitute for the Blind, Deaf, and Dumb (now the Florida School for the
Deaf and Blind). In addition, a mental institution was established in Chat-
tahoochee.

Politically the Democrats were still dominant in state government at the
beginning of the 1900s. Blacks were legally enfranchised but were being
eliminated from the political process through various devices (Florida

used the poll tax). The blacks of the 1900s had not been born into slavery and were not satisfied simply to be free; they wanted to be actively involved in all aspects of their communities. The reaction was a series of race riots, the worst taking place in the northern part of the state. There was great danger for blacks who pushed for civil rights in Florida during this period; the state averaged about fifteen lynchings a year around the turn of the century, many of them linked to racial unrest. Faced with exclusion from equal participation in the white world, blacks constructed their own churches, schools, banks, theaters, and professional groups. The rise of an economy and social system on the other side of the color line was an important development throughout the South during this time.

The role of the automobile, which was to become an important influence on life in Florida, began to emerge early in the 1900s. Automobile tours began at a major city in the North or Midwest and came to Florida as caravans. Newspapers all over the country covered the tours, and people began to realize that one could get to Florida by automobile from places like Chicago, Cincinnati, and New York City. There were still few satisfactory roads in Florida; many were just ruts through the sand. The state initiated some maintenance of highways in 1915, and year by year the automobile opened the state to the whole eastern half of the nation. There were also important developments in air transportation in Florida at this time. The first recorded night flight took place in 1911 and the first passenger flight in 1914, both in Tampa.

World War I started in Europe in the summer of 1914, but the United States did not become involved until April 1917. Military training sites, especially for aviators, were built in Florida because the climate was suitable for year-round flying. The state did not share much in the way of war contracts since it still was not industrialized, but did obtain some small contracts for shipbuilding at places like Pensacola, Jacksonville, and St. Andrews Bay. Florida's citrus crop had only limited application for food purposes in the war. Sugar was scarce, so there was a rush program to put some Florida land into sugarcane production.

After the war, Florida once again experienced change, with more and more tourists coming into the state. In 1916, Congress had passed the National Highway Act, authorizing federal funds to assist states and thus beginning the national highway system. Under Governor Sidney Catts's administration, license tags became a requirement for automobiles, and the income was used for county road building. During his term the legislature also passed the first compulsory school attendance law and several regulations for insurance companies doing business in the state. Another significant development was the horde of land developers who descended on Florida. With the popularity of the automobile, it had become com-

The L. D. Hodge family before a family quilt in the early 1900s in Sarasota County. (By permission of Photographic Collection of State Archives, Florida Bureau of Archives and Records Management, Department of State.)

monplace for people to vacation in Florida, and many decided to remain permanently. By the end of World War I, another substantial growth spurt was under way.

American women still were not working away from their homes in large numbers in the early 1900s; housekeeping and family care consumed most of their time. The economy and easy availability of purchased bedclothes, especially blankets, through large merchandisers like Sears-Roebuck contributed to a waning interest in quilting and other handwork during these years. In addition, the involvement of the United States in World War I led women to shift their efforts to activities like sewing and knitting items needed for American troops. Florida women continued to make quilts, although on a lesser scale. They still made decorative crazy quilts as well as utilitarian quilts that could be made without the purchase of new fabrics.

◆ ◆ ◆

An unusual quilt made around the turn of the century combines dramatic black sections set diagonally with colorful strips of crazy patchwork (Plate 48). It was made in Arthur, Ontario, Canada, by Marie Landis, the aunt of the quilt's current owner, Eleanor Landis of Pensacola, Florida; it was brought to Florida in 1986. Marie was born in Severin Bridge, Ontario, in 1891. In 1919 she married Lewis Landis and lived on a rustic farm, baking,

PLATE 48. *Crazy quilt. Made*
[by] Marie Landis in Arthur,
[On]tario, Canada, about 1900.
[Di]mensions; 70" × 71";
[mi]xed-fiber fabric top; pieced by
[ha]nd and machine; tied; black
[pri]nt cotton backing.

gardening, canning, caring for chickens, and doing handwork. The summers were busy with farming chores, and the winters were cold and difficult. The warm kitchen of the farmhouse was the family gathering place, and Marie did most of her sewing there in the evenings. She used scraps from family clothing to make the much-needed bed covers.

Lucile H. Lovelady of Ocala, Florida, is the owner of a colorful crazy quilt ornamented by unusually beautiful, greatly detailed embroidery (Plate 49). It was made by Rebecca de Yampert Taylor (1857–1942) in Archer, Florida, about 1900. Rebecca was born in Greensboro, Alabama, married in Archer in 1886, and lived there most of her married life. It was fashionable in her young adult years for women to make decorative throws, and she made this one from family clothing remnants and men's ties. Rebecca's husband was a carpenter who built their home and also her large quilting frame, which she kept in their living room.

Plate 50 shows an example of the traditional and popular Log Cabin pattern in the Barn Raising arrangement of blocks. It is owned by Eleanor Maloney, Atlantic Beach, Florida, and was made about 1900 by her grandmother, Charlotta Hagen (c. 1840–1920), in Brooklyn, New York.

A scrap quilt in the Barbara Frietchie Star pattern (Plate 51), made in the early 1900s in Brooker, Bradford County, Florida, by Nancy Crosby Gainey (1888–1968), is owned by her daughter, Lottie Raulerson of Okeechobee, Florida. Nancy was born in Brooker and as a child learned to quilt from her mother. She married a farmer in Bradford County and raised seven children. Her quilting was done for practical purposes, and she worked on her quilts in the evenings and at other leisure moments, using scraps from family clothing as well as a variety of printed feed sacks.

...becca de Yampert Taylor
...d David Taylor with their
...ghter Mary Elizabeth in
...t of their Archer, Florida,
...e, in 1895 (opposite).

PLATE 49. *Crazy quilt. Made
by Rebecca de Yampert Taylor
in Archer, Florida, about 1900.
Dimensions, 70½" × 80"; top
made of a variety of fabrics; no*

*batting; pieced by hand and
sewing machine; bordered with
a ruffle; dark blue cotton
backing.*

PLATE 50. *Log Cabin, Barn Raising setting. Made by Charlotta Hagen about 1900 in Brooklyn, New York. Dimensions, 67" × 82½"; silk top; pieced by hand with blocks set by machine; hand-quilted in channel pattern; cotton batting; silk backing.*

PLATE 51. *Barbara Frietchie Star. Made by Nancy Crosby Gainey in Brooker, Bradford County, Florida, in the early 1900s. Dimensions, 64" × 84"; cotton top; pieced by machine; hand-quilted in clamshell pattern; cotton batting; cotton print backing.*

Nancy Crosby Gainey.

PLATE 52. *Commemorative quilt for the Pan American Exposition in Buffalo, New York (1901). Maker of quilt top* unknown; *remainder of quilt made by Mrs. Griggers of Milton, Florida. Dimensions, 59" × 69"; cotton muslin top;* *pieced by machine; hand-embroidered; hand-quilted in straight line pattern; cotton batting; cotton backing.*

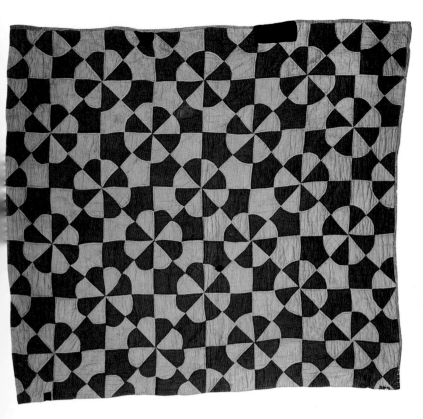

PLATE 53. *Hearts and Gizzards. Made by Ida Henderson Shuler about 1907 in Walton County, Florida. Dimensions, 72" × 80"; cotton top; pieced by hand; hand-quilted; cotton batting with seeds; cotton backing.*

Ida Henderson Shuler.

Julia Wernicke of Pensacola, Florida, owns an unusual red-on-white commemorative quilt made in 1901 for the Pan American Exposition in Buffalo, New York (Plate 52). Julia purchased the top and does not know the name of the person who embroidered and pieced it. She added the feather quilting over the seams; Mrs. Maggie Griggers of Milton, Florida, completed the quilting. The blocks include one picturing President William McKinley and his wife.

A self-sufficient woman with wide-ranging interests, Ida Henderson Shuler (1887–1972), made a Hearts and Gizzards quilt (Plate 53) in Walton County, Florida, about 1907; the quilt now belongs to her daughter, Jean Shuler Martinec, of DeFuniak Springs, Florida. Ida was born in Walton County, Florida, and learned to quilt at about age ten from her mother. When she was sixteen, Ida married Gary Lee Shuler, who worked in the turpentine industry, an important one in northwest Florida at that time, and was also a game warden and farmer. Gardening and canning were among Ida's favorite activities—she worked year-round to prepare canned vegetables for the county fair, and she won many blue ribbons. During the Depression years, Ida and the local Home Demonstration agent, Eloise McGriff, perfected a delicious fruit drink called blueberry nectar. They bottled the drinks and sold them for five cents each. Even at this price, however, only a few people could afford to buy them.

Ida also loved to sew and crochet, but her special love was quilting, on her frame suspended from the ceiling in the front room of her home. Often friends would gather and visit as they quilted. She usually worked on her quilts on rainy days, at night after her other housework was done, and in the winter when outside activities were limited. At one time Ida was responsible for running a gristmill, and she worked on her quilts to pass the time between customers. Most of her patterns and designs were gathered from neighbors and relatives. Ida made her quilts for keeping warm, and she gave many to her children, to needy people of the community, and sometimes to those who had suffered house fires. The quilt pictured in this book was made for her son, Arnold Shuler, and his name is embroidered on the corner. The Shulers grew the cotton used in this quilt, and Ida carded it herself to go into the quilt as batting. She continued to live a busy and productive life near DeFuniak Springs until her death at age eighty-five.

An Irish Chain quilt owned by Rosa Stone Walker of Glen St. Mary, Florida, was made by her mother, Mary Lavinia Rhoden Stone, in Sanderson, Florida, in the early 1900s (Plate 54). Mary was born in 1869 into a pioneer Florida family that settled in Baker County, where they were always active in church and other community activities. They farmed for a living and also owned and operated a general store and the county cotton gin. The Rhodens lived part-time in Sanderson, Florida, once the county seat of rural Baker County. Mary learned to quilt at age fifteen, taught by her mother. Using sample materials from fabric companies and scraps left from sewing for the family, she made quilts both in traditional patterns and in original designs.

In 1884, Mary married William Henry Stone, Jr., a farmer and merchant. The Stones lived in the Cuyler community of northwest Baker County, where Mary did handwork in her spare time—sewing, crochet, and embroidery in addition to quilting.

Evelyn Davidson of Bonifay, Florida, owns an Ocean Wave quilt (Plate 55) made by her grandmother, Martha Ann Gracey Elmore Womble (1868–1937), about 1913 in Jackson County, Florida. Gracey was born in Jackson County and learned to quilt early in life from other family members—mother, aunts, and grandmother. She married Henry Franklin Womble, a farmer, in 1887, and raised six children.

Gracey's quilting exemplified her devotion to her family's comfort. She used a homemade quilt frame suspended from the rafters in a big room of the old Womble homestead. Patterns for quilts were handed down from one generation of her family to another, and she used cotton scraps from family clothing projects to make her quilts. Women of the period often

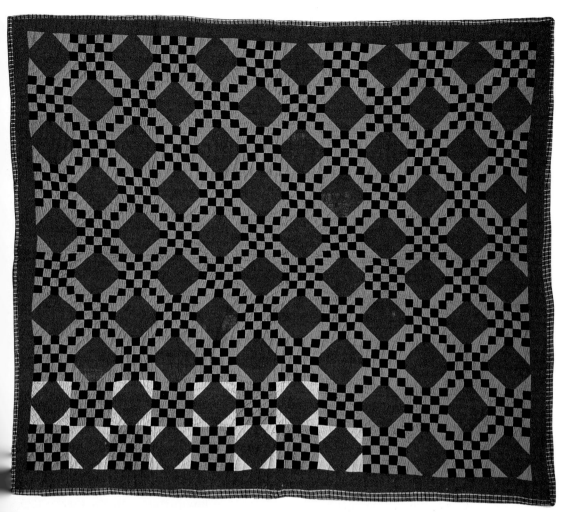

PLATE 54. *Irish Chain. Made by Mary Lavinia Rhoden Stone in the early 1900s in Sanderson, Florida. Dimensions, 66" × 75"; cotton top; pieced by hand; hand-quilted in fan pattern; cotton batting; cotton backing.*

Mary Lavinia Rhoden Stone and baby Ezra.

PLATE 55 *(opposite). Ocean Wave. Made by Martha Ann Gracey Elmore Womble about 1913 in Jackson County, Florida. Dimensions, 58" × 78"; cotton top; pieced by hand; quilted by hand in clamshell pattern; cotton batting; cotton print backing.*

Martha Ann Gracey Elmore Womble and Henry Franklin Womble.

took clothing apart to remake it for other family members as another means of recycling their fabric to the fullest.

Gracey Womble is remembered by family members as a strict person but one who did much to help others. On numerous occasions she took into her home people who had suffered misfortunes in life, and she always kept a supply of homemade teacakes and fresh milk (kept cool in her well) as refreshments for anyone who stopped by. A family story is that her pastor walked twenty miles to preach at the New Home Baptist church and always visited with Gracey on the way to enjoy the teacakes from her pie safe with a glass of cool milk. She lived most of her life at the Womble homestead in Walton County, and she passed on her interest and skills in sewing to her daughters. This quilt was passed on to her daughter, Ella Womble Smith, and then to her granddaughter Evelyn.

A Jacob's Ladder quilt owned by Constance M. O'Neill of Cocoa, Florida, contains the work of three generations in her family (Plate 56). The quilt was pieced in 1913 in Montgomery County, Pennsylvania, by Jacob and Mary Ann Landis Long, Constance's great-grandparents; the center section was quilted by Ida S. Long, her grandmother; and Constance added the borders, backing, and binding in Cocoa, Florida, in 1986. Jacob S. Long was a carpenter who also worked in a creamery, and his wife, Mary, was a seamstress and homemaker. They were married in 1891 and lived in Earlington, Montgomery County, Pennsylvania, where they worked to-

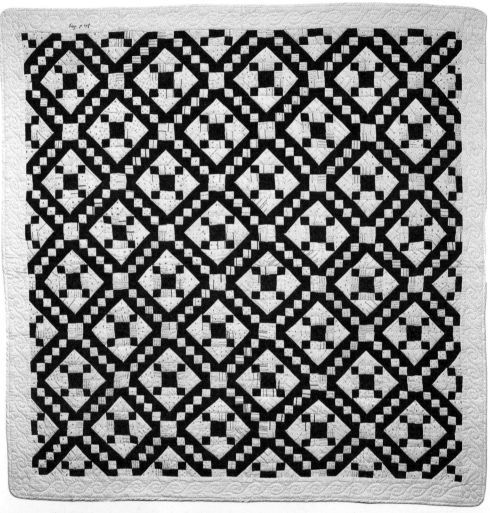

Mary Landis Long.

·Jacob S. Long (left) and Jacob
and Mary's son Robert.

PLATE 56. *Jacob's Ladder.*
Made by Jacob S. and Mary
Ann Landis Long, Ida S.
Long, and Constance O'Neill.
Top pieced in 1913 in Pennsyl-
vania and remainder of quilt
completed in 1986. Dimen-
sions, 71½" × 74"; cotton top;
pieced by machine; fine hand-
quilting in channel and ocean
waves patterns; polyester bat-
ting; white muslin backing.

gether to make quilts for family bedding. As a seamstress Mary made men's shirts, and the white pieces in this quilt were leftovers from those projects.

Sarah Melvine Vickers Tucker (1856–1937) made the quilt in Plate 57 sometime before 1916 at her home in Aaron, Florida, in Wakulla County; it now belongs to her great-granddaughter, Helen Adams Strickland of Crawfordville, Florida. The quilt has a large block in the center surrounded by randomly pieced strips and was called the "Puzzle Fast" quilt by the family. Sarah was born in Pin Hooks, Florida, married Alfred Lawrence Tucker in 1879, and raised four children. Her granddaughter, Gladys Griner Adams, can remember living with her grandmother when she was about eight years old. Sarah's sisters, sisters-in-law, and friends came one day a week to quilt with her. She made a quilt for each of her grandchildren, and gave the Puzzle Fast quilt to Gladys when she was ten years old.

Directly in front of the old railroad depot in Aaron, the Tuckers had a general merchandise store which was an important part of their lives; local fishermen and oystermen supplied the market for the store. Sarah ran the store so that Alfred could run the farm. Sarah also had time for cooking that is still fondly remembered by her family. Gladys recalls arriving in Aaron on the train, then riding in the surrey from the depot to the farm. As they drove down the long driveway, she could smell the food—collard greens, fried chicken, and pound cake.

Similar in construction to the Puzzle Fast quilt is a Block Medallion quilt (Plate 58) owned by Bea Fleming Clarke of Tallahassee, Florida, made about 1918 in Jacksonville, Florida, by her grandmother, Mary Louisa (Lula) Augusta Wyche James Jackson (1857–1935). Lula Jackson was born into a slave family in Madison County, Florida, in 1857. She was eight years old at the end of the Civil War and told her children and grandchildren about the dancing and singing that took place when the slaves were freed. Lula and other family members managed somehow to survive the years after they left the plantation where they had lived. Later she married Howard Arthur James, and they had three children. In 1881 Howard was killed during the civil rights violence in North Florida. In 1886 she married John Jackson, who already had several children of his own, and they had two more children.

Later in her life Lula lived in Jacksonville with her daughter Edie Jackson Fleming. She did a great deal of sewing and mending and also made knitted lace, which she used to trim pillowcases made from flour sacks. Most of Lula's quilting was done after she moved to Jacksonville; she especially enjoyed quilting on the front porch while she visited with family and friends. She maintained a family rag bag to supply material for her quilt tops. She used whatever was handy for batting in her utilitarian quilts—

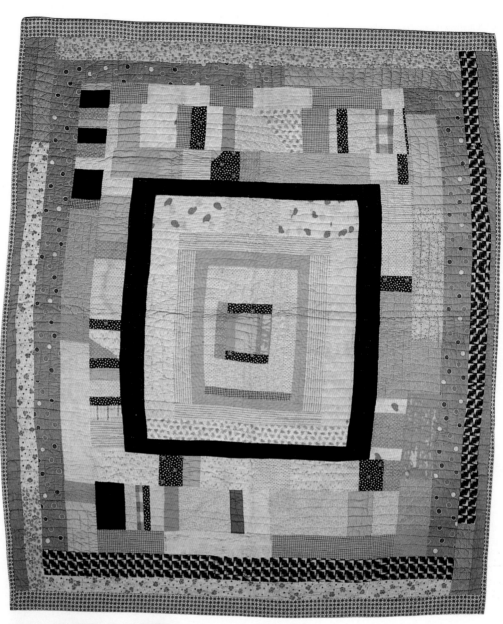

PLATE 57. *"Puzzle Fast."*
Made by Sarah Melvine Vickers
Tucker in Aaron, Florida,
before 1916. Dimensions, 69
½" × 81½"; cotton top; pieced
by hand; channel-quilted by
hand; thick cotton batting;
striped cotton backing.

Sarah Melvine Vickers Tucker
and Alfred Lawrence Tucker.

PLATE 58. *Block Medallion quilt. Made by Mary Louisa Augusta Wyche James Jackson in Jacksonville, Florida, about 1918. Dimensions, 64" × 77"; cotton top; pieced by hand; quilted by hand in fan pattern; woven coverlet batting; white cotton backing.*

Mary Louisa Augusta (Lula) Wyche James Jackson.

another old quilt, a blanket, a coverlet, or even worn underwear. She was proud of saying that she never purchased anything to use in making a quilt. The Block Medallion quilt incorporates several design aspects that reflect African textile construction techniques and often are characteristic of African-American quilts, such as pieced-strip construction and random color choice (Horton, p. 44). Other quilts registered during the project, such as Sarah Tucker's "Puzzle Fast" quilt, include similar characteristics although they were not made by African-American quilters. Lula Jackson is just one example of the remarkable women who began literally with nothing when they were freed from slavery and managed against all odds to build successful lives and make meaningful contributions to their worlds.

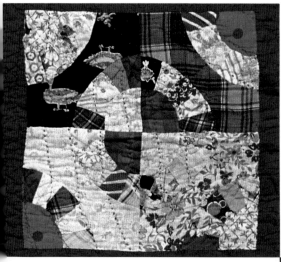

The Roaring
Twenties and
the Depression
(1920–1940)

♦   ♦   ♦

THE MOST SIGNIFICANT ROARING that occurred in Florida during the 1920s was the sound of automobile engines as increasing numbers of the American public came into the state. For a long time Florida's railroad hotels and resorts had been the playgrounds of the very rich—now many people from different economic classes were coming to Florida by automobile. Ford's Model T was economical enough for many Americans to own. A trip to Florida was not only an opportunity to get away from the cold weather. It was a chance to visit a fantasyland of white sandy beaches, palm trees, and blue waters—and you could go in the family automobile. When they traveled by car, these visitors of moderate means could take along a tent, a camp stove, and canned foods and live out of their autos. Florida's "tin-can campers" of the twenties went into many new areas of the state, and many became permanent residents.

Florida's population increased from a million to about a million and a half during the twenties. The cities taking shape along the water, especially Miami and those around Tampa Bay, were the areas of greatest growth. Some parts of central Florida, the Lakeland area in particular, owed their growth to access by automobile. The northern portion of the state, however, did not experience comparable development.

The increasing importance of the automobile's role in Florida's development was reflected in the beginning of a modern road system in the state during the twenties. Many of the visitors and new residents of the state— as well as many other people who simply read about Florida—became interested in land speculation. During the land boom that occurred in South Florida in the mid-twenties, Florida real estate was sold and resold and profits soared.

Following the period of accelerated growth, Florida experienced a series of natural and man-made disasters. Prohibition had a strong effect in

Florida; the state became a center for rum-running from Cuba and the Bahamas. Also during this time Tampa became a center for narcotics smuggling. These developments led to an increased crime rate in some areas. Fraud in the banking community precipitated a major panic that was accelerated by the rapidly declining land values. About half of the state and national banks in Florida failed. The land bubble burst after 1925, when money and credit were exhausted and banks and investors ceased to trust paper-millionaire developers. This financial collapse was followed closely by a major hurricane in 1926 and another in 1928. By the time the Great Depression came to the rest of the nation, people in Florida were already facing hard times.

The still dominant Democratic Party made good on its promises of road construction. The state government enacted tax shelters for the wealthy, initiated wildlife conservation programs, and continued to show interest in draining the Everglades. Gandy Bridge over Tampa Bay was opened in 1924, the longest automobile toll bridge in the world. The Seaboard Railroad pioneered a new class of streamliner passenger trains, and Florida had one of the first, the Silver Meteor, which traveled from New York City to Tampa and Miami. So, in spite of some rather spectacular setbacks and an emerging economic depression, Florida reached the close of the 1920s having made greater gains in population than in any time before (Tebeau, p. 377).

Florida was in a depression three years before the stock market crash of 1929. The state's apparent prosperity in the early 1920s was selective—not everyone had participated in the boom. Farmers were in a depressed state throughout the decade, and the budding tourism industry faced serious difficulties. The Depression in Florida was different from the rest of the country. Since the state was not industrialized, there were no shanty towns or long breadlines as in northern cities. In the rural areas of Florida, if the family could stay on the farm, they could at least eat well. However, many families were losing their land for nonpayment of taxes, and if the land was lost any sharecroppers living on it were forced off also. There was a dramatic decline in property values because Florida real estate had been so overvalued during the boom period.

In Florida most of the Depression relief efforts were handled by cities, counties, and private groups. Eventually, racetrack betting under state supervision was approved to raise the needed funds, but it was not enough. It was not until Franklin Roosevelt's New Deal that Florida was able to obtain substantial assistance from the federal level. In 1935 the legislature took some of the first steps toward state relief for the counties and also authorized $1 million for public work projects, chiefly roads. By 1936 things were definitely looking better for Florida—tourism was on the increase again, and it appeared that the worst was over. In 1938 the overseas highway to Key West was completed, and nearly three million tourists crossed it by automobile in its first year. The state still was short of funds, however, and in 1940 new alcohol and cigarette taxes were passed and a gasoline tax enacted to be used for road construction.

By the late 1920s more and more women in Florida and across the nation were working away from their homes, primarily because of the economic needs of their families; and more were receiving college degrees. Before women gained the power of the vote, their only political clout came from banding together to support reform movements. With the passage of the Nineteenth Amendment in 1920, Florida women not only voted, they also began to run for political office—and to be elected. Their role expanded to every area of life, including politics and business. Although two women were candidates for the Florida House of Representatives in 1922, it was not until 1928 that the first woman was elected to a statewide office. In that year Mamie Eaton Greene of Monticello was elected to the state railroad commission. Beginning in 1929, Ruth Bryan Owen, the daughter of William Jennings Bryan, served two terms as the first woman to represent Florida in the U.S. Congress.

◆　　　　　　　　　　◆　　　　　　　　　　◆

Throughout the twentieth century interest in the art of quilt making has waxed and waned. Revivals of interest often followed war or economic turmoil, and the Depression inspired a mild revival because so many people were concerned with thrift and economy. Women everywhere were encouraged to sew. Quilting kits were advertised in magazines and newspapers, quilting bee contests were promoted, quilting patterns were reproduced in the print media, and quilt contests and exhibitions were held throughout the country. With their patriotism and interest in handicrafts aroused, more and more people began to appreciate quilts and to purchase them for their beauty and historical significance (Orlofsky, pp. 62–64).

The FQH Project registered quilts made all across the state during the twenties and thirties—from Milton in the western Florida Panhandle over to Jacksonville on the Atlantic coast and south to Miami. Most Florida quilters were still producing primarily for family bedding and were using whatever fabrics they had available. During these decades most quilt-makers in Florida created hand-sewn patchwork quilt tops using traditional patterns.

Margaret Hancock Mizell (1859–1937) made a traditional Trenton Block Variation quilt in the 1920s in Tarpon Springs, Florida (Plate 59). She was

A group of Columbia County women quilting on a frame in the 1940s. (By permission of Photographic Collection of State Archives, Florida Bureau of Archives and Records Management, Department of State.)

born in Dixie, Florida, into a family that had settled in Pasco County in the early 1830s. Her mother taught her to quilt in her early childhood, using scraps from family clothing and fabric samples from stores. Margaret married a farmer and did much of her quilting in her home in Tarpon Springs, often working from her own designs. Her granddaughter, Helen T. Thompson of St. Petersburg, Florida, now owns this quilt.

During this period quilting was sometimes used as occupational therapy in hospital settings; the quilt shown in Plate 60 was made by patients in the state mental hospital in Chattahoochee, Florida, in 1925. The appliquéd Poinsettia quilt was made as a retirement gift for Mrs. Willie Kirkland when she left the hospital. She gave the quilt to Evelyn Coleman in 1975, and in 1985 it was given to Lynn M. Smith of Evinston, Florida, its current owner.

PLATE 59. *Trenton Block
Variation. Made by Margaret
Hancock Mizell in the 1920s
in Tarpon Springs, Florida.
Dimensions, 64" × 76½";
cotton top; pieced by hand and
machine; hand-quilted in fan
and other patterns; cotton batting with seeds; ecru cotton
backing.*

PLATE 60. *Poinsettia. Made by patients at the Florida State Mental Hospital in Chattahoochee, Florida, in 1925.*

Dimensions, 78″ × 93″; unbleached cotton muslin top; appliquéd by hand; hand-quilted in echo and floral pat-

terns with background quilted in diamond grid; cotton batting; unbleached cotton muslin backing.

Sarah Florence Hinote Mitchell.

Thomas G. and Pauline M. Lane of Cocoa Beach, Florida, are the owners of a multicolored Dutch Rose quilt (Plate 61) that was made by Thomas's grandmother, Sarah Florence Hinote Mitchell (1860–1948) in Milton, Florida, in 1925. Sarah was born in Santa Rosa County and lived most of her life in Milton. She married David Mitchell in 1883, and they raised four children. David was the long-time sheriff of Santa Rosa County, and at that time living quarters for the sheriff and his family were in the county jail building. Sarah Mitchell's life was busy with raising children and chickens, vegetable and flower gardening, reading, and quilting. She learned to quilt at age thirty-five, self-taught. She often created her own patterns and used some traditional patterns to make quilts from clothing scraps and flour sacks. This quilt is one of many that she made until her eyesight would no longer permit.

Quilts made in soft pastel colors were especially popular during the twenties, and an example of this type is a Lone Star quilt made by Martha Mount Folmar in Laurel Hill, Florida, about 1927–28 (Plate 62). Martha was born in 1864 in Pike County, Alabama. She married George Folmar, who farmed, ran a store, and operated a naval stores business as well. They lived most of their married life in Laurel Hill. Martha taught all her daughters to quilt. She purchased fabric especially for her quilt making, and this quilt was one of several that Martha made in the same color combination, with a different color as the background for each. This Lone Star was made as a wedding gift for Martha's son and is now owned by her granddaughter Lacy Folmar Bullard of Tallahassee, Florida.

Another product of the late 1920s is a quilt in the Robbing Peter to Pay Paul pattern (Plate 63), owned by Lois and Joseph Raymond Henschen of

PLATE 61. *Dutch Rose.* Made by Sarah Florence Hinote Mitchell in 1925 in Milton, Florida. Dimensions, 66" × 77"; cotton top; pieced by hand; hand-quilted in fan pattern; cotton batting; natural muslin backing.

PLATE 62. *Lone Star. Made by Martha Mount Folmar in Laurel Hill, Florida, between 1927 and 1928. Dimensions, 71" × 81½"; cotton top; pieced by hand; fine hand-quilting in outline, parallel, and fan patterns; cotton batting; pink cotton backing.*

PLATE 63. *Robbing Peter to Pay Paul. Made by Edna Luella Knight Iserman in 1928 in Killarney, Florida. Dimensions, 80" × 94"; cotton top; pieced by hand and repaired by sewing machine; hand-quilted; thin cotton batting; off-white cotton backing.*

Edna Luella Knight Iserman.

St. Cloud, Florida. This graphic quilt was made by Edna Luella (Luddie) Knight Iserman, Joseph's grandmother, in Killarney, Florida, in 1928. Luddie was born in Indiana but lived most of her life in Overbrook, Kansas. At age twenty-four she married Henry Iserman, a dentist. Due to Dr. Iserman's ill health, the family moved to Florida about 1900 and settled in Payola in Seminole County to raise vegetables. As soon as Henry's health improved, the family returned to Kansas. When he retired in 1928, the Isermans returned to Florida, this time to an orange grove at Killarney, on Lake Apopka in Orange County, where Luddie lived until her death in 1944. With seven children, Luddie was always busy but found some time for needlework. This quilt was made for Joseph when he was six years old.

A brilliant jewel-toned version of the traditional Log Cabin quilt (Plate 64) was made in 1928 in Miami, Florida, and is now owned by Dempsey Creary of Miami Springs, Florida, and Miriam Turner Barbee of Gulf Breeze, Florida. It was made by Bertha Amos Creary (1871–1959), Dempsey's mother and Miriam's grandmother. Bertha was the daughter of early Florida settlers, and her birthplace, Milton, Florida, was named for her great-grandfather, Dr. Milton Amos. She began quilting at age thirteen, learning the skills from her mother, Nancy Amos. In 1889 Bertha married Harry Lee Creary, a carpenter, and they raised seven children. The Crearys operated the Exchange Hotel in Milton and the Bagdad Inn in Bagdad, Florida, in the 1930s. She was well known for the wonderful meals at the inn and even cultivated a large garden so they would always have fresh vegetables for the table.

Gail and Kenneth Kirkland of Macclenny, Florida, are the owners of a quilt made in 1930 in Macclenny by Ruth Cone (1892–1972), Kenneth's grandmother. The quilt is pieced in the Dove at the Window pattern (Plate 65). Ruth was a librarian and seamstress who moved to Macclenny when she married Branch Cone, an attorney, in 1913.

A descendant of two pioneer Florida families, Sadie Mae Thrift Yarborough (1910–83), made a Double Fan Variation quilt (Plate 66) in Baker County, Florida, in the 1930s; it is now owned by her grandson Ken Sands of Glen St. Mary, Florida. Sadie was born at the Thrift family home north of Macclenny, the daughter of Moses Thrift and Laura Hunter Thrift. Their home had an old well beside the road where travelers often stopped for cool fresh water. Beside that well Sadie met her future husband, Corbett Yarbrough, a furniture and appliance store owner in Macclenny. When she married him in 1928, Sadie became the mother of Corbett's four children, aged one through five, and the two of them had five more children.

Caring for others was a role well suited to Sadie's personality, and she is remembered as a compassionate woman with a great zest for life. Her home was a warm place, crowded with family and friends enjoying her

PLATE 64. *Log Cabin, Straight Furrows setting. Made by Bertha Amos Creary in Miami, Florida, in 1928. Dimensions, 78" × 88"; top made of a variety of fabrics; pieced by machine; tied; rayon backing.*

Bertha Amos Creary and Harry Lee Creary.

Ruth Cone's home in Mac-
clenny, Florida.

Ruth Cone.

PLATE 65. *Dove at the Window. Made by Ruth Cone in
1930 in Macclenny, Florida.
Dimensions, 68" × 80½";
cotton top; pieced by hand;
hand-quilted in floral and
parallel line patterns; cotton
batting; white cotton backing.*

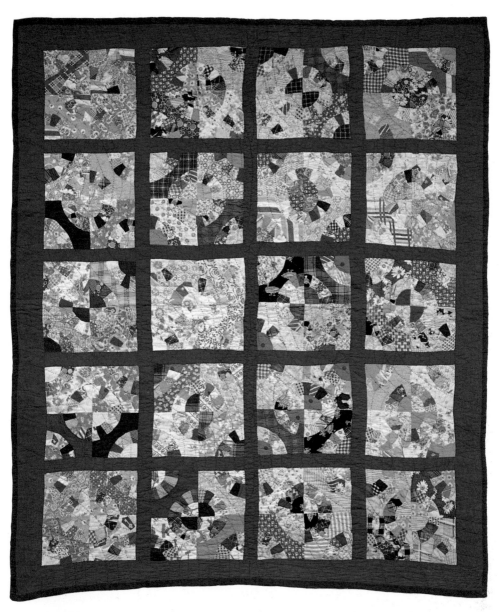

PLATE 66. *Double Fan Varia-*
tion. Made by Sadie Mae
Thrift Yarborough in Baker
County, Florida, in the 1930s.
Dimensions, 62" × 73"; cot-
ton top; pieced by hand; hand-
quilted in fan pattern; cotton
batting; blue cotton backing.

Sadie Mae Thrift Yarborough.

Mark and Blanche Burgher.

hospitality and wonderful meals. She and her sister frequently congregated in their homes for quilting, and the quilts she made are still being used by her children and grandchildren.

Sadie's granddaughter, Sanella Ray Sands Lindsey, remembers her as a child's idea of a perfect person—everything a little girl could love and admire. They did household chores side by side with the child following her every move and hanging on her every word. "We went to the grocery store together, to 'Miss Sippie's' so Grandma could get her hair done, fishing, church activities, Lion's Club, and any other places her various interests took her. . . . From this constant following of Grandma, I received a nickname—I was called my Grandma's Shadow and that is one nickname I am proud to have. . . . She did not do for other people so that she will be rewarded for it, she did things because it was her nature."

Blanche Burgher of Ocala, Florida, still has a sixteen-patch quilt that she made in 1930 and aptly named the "Depression Prints" quilt (Plate 67). It was pieced in Florida and quilted in Illinois. Blanche was born in 1909 in Coulterville, Illinois, and married Mark Burgher in 1933. During some of their years in Illinois she and Mark ran a gas station, and he also worked for a railway mail service. She had a long career with Sears in Chicago and retired in 1969.

During the late 1920s and early 1930s Blanche accumulated the fabrics for this quilt. Once she stood in line to get scraps from a dress factory, and she ordered some of the fabric from Sears and Wards catalogs. She began piecing the quilt on a family trip to Florida, camping in a state park north of Tampa. The Burghers had always spent vacations in Florida, and in 1969 they moved there. Blanche has made a quilt for each of her three children and is planning to make one for each of her seven grandchildren.

LeNora Tompkins Collins (1867–1953) made a bright red and green on white appliquéd quilt in the 1930s in Webster, Florida, which is said to be her original design (Plate 68). It is the last of many quilts that she made

PLATE 67. "Depression Prints" in sixteen-patch blocks. Made by Blanche Burgher in Florida and Illinois in 1930. Dimensions, 81" × 99"; cotton top; pieced by hand; hand-quilted in diagonal lines; polyester batting; white polycotton backing.

PLATE 68. *Floral appliqué. Made by LeNora Tompkins Collins in the 1930s in Webster, Florida. Dimensions, 70" × 93"; cotton top; hand-appliquéd; hand-quilted in outline patterns; cotton batting; white cotton backing.*

LeNora Tompkins Collins.

and was owned by her granddaughter Elizabeth Collins Carter, of Jacksonville, Florida, at the time of the Florida Quilt Heritage registration. Elizabeth donated the quilt to the Museum of Florida History in the summer of 1989.

LeNora was born in Providence, Florida, in the Starke area, and moved to Sumter County by wagon when she was eight. The Tompkins family settled near Riverland in south Sumter County and later moved to Linden, Florida. In 1885 she married David Collins and they moved about three miles south of Webster. Her wedding present was a new home, a large frame house constructed from lumber cut on their farm. In this home she raised her family and the younger children from her husband's first marriage. David, one of Florida's earliest citrus growers, was a veteran of the Seminole wars and the Civil War.

LeNora was a charter member of the Webster Methodist Church, established in 1885. She was a progressive person and was among the first in her community to acquire new labor-saving devices such as a refrigerator, hot water heater, radio, and electric stove. She made quilts for each of her granddaughters, piecing them all by hand. Soon after her husband's death in 1900, LeNora moved into town, where she lived the rest of her years.

A beautiful pastel quilt from the 1930s, the English Flower Pot quilt in Plate 69 is owned by Marion Mann of Pinellas Park, Florida, and was made by her grandmother, Hattie M. Kibby Jennings (1880–1964), in St. Petersburg, Florida. Hattie was born in Emporia, Kansas, and married Gordon Burnet Jennings there in 1900. They had two daughters, but in 1931 Hattie was widowed and the family moved to Florida. Hattie had always sewed for her whole family, and after the move to Florida she had more time available and became an avid quilter. She especially enjoyed appliqué work and did beautiful patchwork as well.

Another scrap quilt from the depression era is the Double Wedding Ring made by Edna Earle McKee in 1931 in Cottondale, Florida (Plate 70). Edna Earle gave the quilt to her sister, Martha L. Pierce of Pensacola, Florida, the current owner. There were nine children in the family, and Edna Earle was the middle child, born in 1914. Their mother was a seamstress who taught Edna Earle to quilt when she was seventeen. She graduated from high school in Cottondale that spring, and since there were no jobs and little entertainment available, she spent a great deal of time quilting and was able to complete the quilt within the three summer months of 1931.

The quilt was made from scraps from clothing their mother had made for the family, and they carded cotton grown by their grandfather for the batting. The family lived in a house with very large rooms; each room had

PLATE 69. *English Flower Pot. Made in the 1930s in St. Petersburg, Florida, by Hattie M. Kibby Jennings. Dimensions, 63" × 77¾"; cotton top; appliquéd by hand and machine; hand-quilted in diamond and parallel line patterns and crosshatch in borders; cotton batting; white cotton backing.*

Hattie M. Kibby Jennings.   *Edna Earle McKee.*

ATE 70. *Double Wedding
*ng. Made by Edna Earle
*Kee in 1931 in Cottondale,
*rida. Dimensions, 78" ×
*; cotton top; pieced by
*chine; hand-quilted in fan
*ern; cotton batting; cotton
slin backing.

four double windows, and Edna Earle worked at a quilting frame suspended from the ceiling in one of the large upstairs rooms. Edna Earle currently lives in Pensacola where she spends her time working with a variety of handwork as well as with her newer interest in creative writing.

A String Star scrap quilt (Plate 71) owned by Sarah L. Speights of Marianna, Florida, was pieced by her mother, Julia Britt Baker (1888–1964), in the 1920s and quilted by Sarah's sister, Adranna Gundrum, in Freeport, Florida, in 1931. Julia learned to quilt at a young age, about ten, and pieced this quilt when she was about thirty-two years old, using scraps from family clothing. Her daughter Sarah describes the construction of the quilt: "She cut over a hundred diamonds out of newspapers. Then she cut up her cloth in strips—we called them strings. She stitched the strings onto the paper diamonds by hand. The colored cloth and plaids came from mine and my sister's dresses. The heavy chambray was the boys' work shirts (everyday) and the stripes were from their Sunday shirts. The gold and gray plaid is from my dress. Mother ordered the red solid cloth from the Walter Field catalog by the yards or by the pound." After the family moved to DeFuniak Springs in 1931, Julia sent the quilt back to Freeport so that Adranna could quilt it.

Willie J. Hutchison, Marianna, Florida, owns an Eight-Pointed or LeMoyne Star quilt (Plate 72) made by her mother, Dellar Hutchison (1888–1939), in Cottondale, Florida, in 1932. This quilt has African-American design characteristics: bold colors, large design elements, and random fabric combinations. Dellar was born in South Carolina but lived most of her life in Jackson County, Florida. Her mother taught her how to sew and make quilts when she was sixteen, and she became a gifted seamstress. According to her daughter, Dellar was the only dressmaker in the community and designed most of the clothing patterns she used. She was employed as a housekeeper also but still found time for quilting. Dellar used dress fabric scraps from her sewing and often found quilt patterns in magazines.

A unique pictorial quilt known as the "Miracle Quilt of Democracy" (Plate 73) was made by Catherine Elizabeth (Kate) Waldron McClenny (c. 1870–1952) in 1932 in Jacksonville Beach, Florida. Kate was married to Carr Bowers McClenny and lived in the Jacksonville area all her life. She taught piano and violin and was always interested in politics. Although this quilt was a totally original design and does not contain any of the traditional design elements popular with quilters of her day, Kate did use the pastel colors in her appliqué and embroidery that were so widely used during this period. She had no previous experience in quilting but managed to complete this quilt in less than a year. While the central theme of the quilt

PLATE 71. *String Star. Pieced by Julia Britt Baker in the 1920s and quilted by Adranna Gundrum in 1931—both in northwest Florida. Dimen-* *sions, 68" × 78½"; cotton top; pieced by hand; quilted by hand; cotton batting; red print cotton backing.*

PLATE 72. *Eight-Pointed Star.*
Made by Dellar Hutchison in
Cottondale, Florida, in 1932.
Dimensions, 78″ × 82″; cot-
ton top; pieced by hand; hand-
quilted in clamshell pattern;
cotton batting; red cotton
backing.

Catherine Elizabeth (Kate)
Waldron McClenny.

PLATE 73. *"Miracle Quilt of Democracy." Made by Catherine Elizabeth (Kate) Waldron McClenny in Jackson-ville Beach, Florida, in 1932. Dimensions, 66½" × 84"; cotton top; appliquéd and embroidered by hand; hand-quilted in parallel and outline patterns; cotton batting; light green cotton backing with pink appliquéd bows.*

is democracy, symbolized by Franklin D. Roosevelt's Little White House, it also incorporates biblical symbols and other facets of life in America.

The quilt was presented before the 1937 Florida legislature and was later exhibited in Jacksonville's Roosevelt and George Washington hotels. Then Senator Claude Pepper liked the quilt so much that he had it displayed at several Florida Democratic party meetings. The mayor and city council of Jacksonville Beach adopted a resolution in 1945 commending Kate for the vision and artistry she employed in the conception and execution of the "Banner of Democracy." Kate dedicated the quilt to the young men who gave their lives in World War II, and it now belongs to the Beaches Area Historical Society in Jacksonville Beach, Florida.

A striking quilt of unusual colors, the George Washington's Plume quilt in Plate 74 is owned by Charlotte Freels Duvall of Miami, Florida. It was made about 1928–32 in Morristown, Tennessee, by Hettie Campbell (1877–1936). Hettie was a highly skilled and dedicated practical nurse who came to stay with the Freels family with the birth of each new baby—she stayed for several months at a time, taking complete charge of the new infant. When the youngest sister was born, Hettie came from her home in Morristown to St. Petersburg, Florida, to take over her care. When the baby was a few months old, the family drove Hettie back to Tennessee.

Hettie made a quilt for each child in the Freels family. Charlotte's mother would provide funds for her to purchase quilting materials and then would purchase the quilt when it was completed. Charlotte recalls that Hettie always included yellow in her bright quilt patterns.

Anna Vircey Miles Bedsole (1898–1983), made a Dresden Plate Variation quilt in 1935–36 in Holmes County, Florida (Plate 75). It is now owned by her daughter, Glyndol Commander, of Ponce de Leon. Born in Darlington, Florida, Vircey was orphaned in childhood and went to live in Walton County with her grandparents. She learned to quilt at age twelve at her grandmother's old quilt frame. They used scraps of fabric left over from making the children's school clothes. Quilts served as bedding for the family, and the women and girls worked on them almost daily.

In 1918 Vircey married Rayford Bedsole in Paxton, Florida, and the couple raised three daughters; they later moved to Ponce de Leon. Vircey taught first grade for many years and also spent some of her leisure time as a volunteer, teaching sewing to youngsters. She was always a dedicated homemaker and was an active member of the Extension Homemakers Club as well as other community organizations. In 1980, when Vircey was eighty-three, she received the honor of being chosen the first Queen of the Collard Festival in Ponce de Leon.

Members of the citrus-packing crew working in the Chandler Davis Packing House in Lakeland, Florida, in 1938 made a friendship quilt which

PLATE 74. *George Washington's Plume. Made about 1928–32 in Morristown, Tennessee, by Hettie Campbell. Dimensions, 74" × 86"; cotton top; appliquéd by hand; quilted by hand in crosshatch pattern; cotton batting; yellow cotton backing.*

Hettie Campbell.

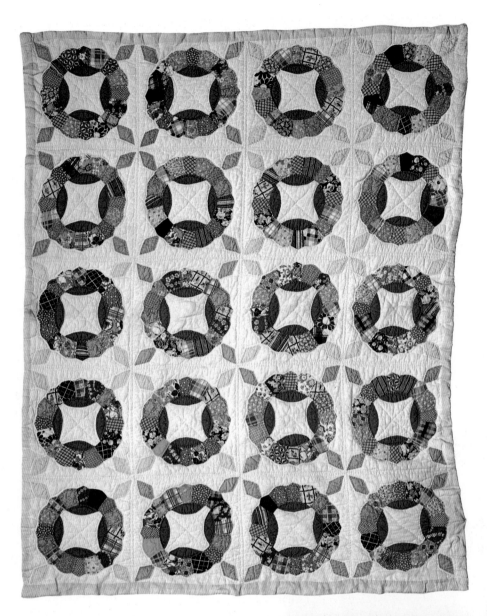

PLATE 75. *Dresden Plate Vari-*
ation. Made by Anna Vircey
Miles Bedsole in 1935–36 in
Holmes County, Florida.
Dimensions, 63" × 78"; cot-
ton top; pieced by hand and
machine; hand-quilted in paral-
lel lines; cotton batting; peach
cotton backing.

Anna Vircey Miles Bedsole.

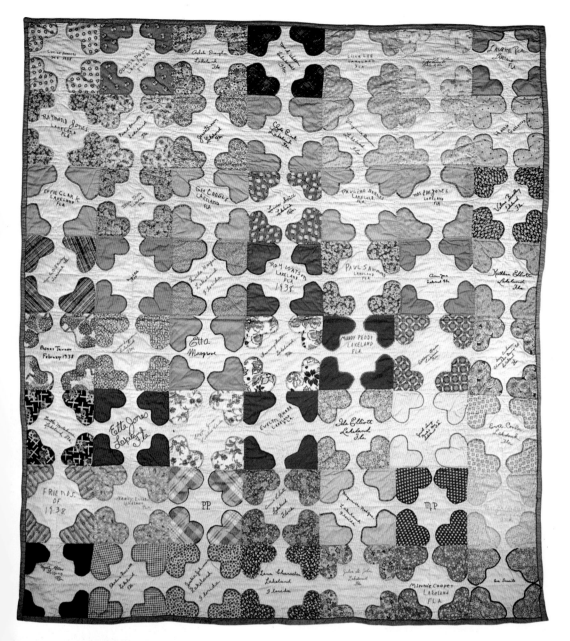

PLATE 76. *Friendship quilt. Made by members of the crew at the Chandler Davis Packing House in Lakeland, Florida, in 1938; now a part of the collection of the Museum of Florida History, Tallahassee. Dimensions, 76″ × 84″; cotton top; appliquéd by hand; hand-embroidered signatures; quilted by hand; cotton batting; cotton backing.*

Effie C. Clark.

PLATE 77. *Floral wreath medley (Oak Leaf and Rose Wreath). Assembled and quilted in 1938 by Averta Atwell Rogers and Lillian d'Elia in Mary-land. Dimensions, 74" × 87"; cotton top; appliquéd by hand; hand-quilted in fan pattern; cotton batting; yellow cotton backing.*

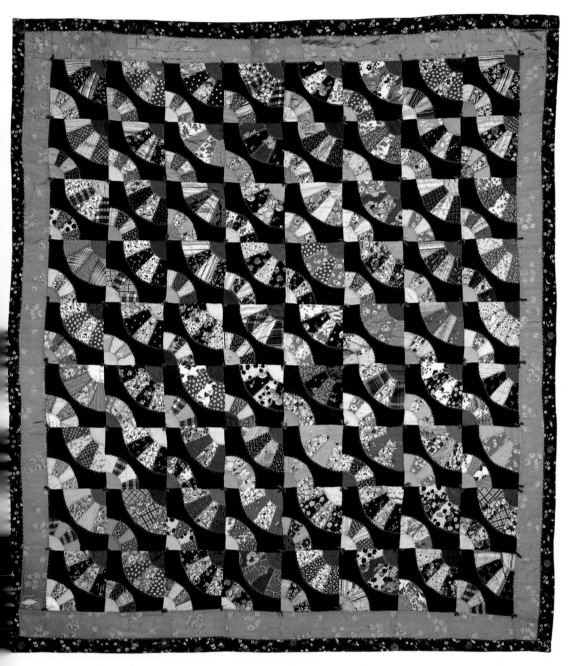

PLATE 78. *Double Fan or Bowtie. Made in Tampa, Florida, about 1940 by Margaret Hill; now a part of the collection of the Museum of Florida History, Tallahassee. Dimensions, 71¹/₄" × 81⁷/₈"; silk, rayon, and cotton top; pieced by hand; hand-embroidered; hand-tied; printed cotton backing.*

is now a part of the collection of the Museum of Florida History (Plate 76). One of the workers, Effie C. Clark, of Lakeland, initiated the project and coordinated construction of the quilt. The women workers made appliquéd blocks from Effie's heart-shaped pattern and embroidered their names on them. Effie made squares for the men and sewed all the blocks together to form the quilt top. At the end of the citrus-packing season a group of the women completed the project in a day-long quilting bee, and the whole crew got together for a chicken dinner to celebrate.

Maria D. Walters, Jacksonville, Florida, owns a quilt that represents the work of two generations in her family and has preserved several antique appliquéd blocks (Plate 77). In 1938 in Maryland, Maria's grandmother, Averta Atwell Rogers, and her mother, Lillian d'Elia, were given blocks done in Oak Leaf and Rose Wreath variations which were said to be fifty years old at the time. The two women purchased yellow cotton fabric and appliquéd the blocks to the background, and Averta then did the quilting.

Averta Rogers (1868–1968) was a homemaker whose husband was a preacher and boatman. She was interested in various types of handwork and had a large quilt frame set up over her dining room table and belonged to a group that quilted in each other's homes. She made quilts for family use, as gifts, and sometimes as commissioned works. Her daughter, Lillian d'Elia (1900–1981), was the wife of a custom tailor and she helped in his shop in addition to raising her two children.

An unusual quilt in the Double Fan or Bowtie pattern that echoes in its fabrics and embroidery the earlier popularity of crazy quilts is shown in Plate 78. It was made in Tampa, Florida, about 1940 by Margaret Hill (1871–1970). Margaret's husband was a carpenter who helped build the original stalls of the Florida State Fair when it was held on the Hillsborough River. She entered many items in the annual fairs, including tablecloths, bedspreads, and quilts. This quilt was entered a number of times and was awarded a first prize each time. It was donated to the Museum of Florida History by Genevieve and Bruce Moeller of Brandon, Florida, in 1984.

World War II
(1941–1945)

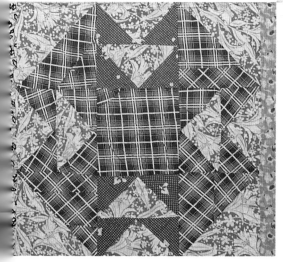

♦   ♦   ♦

THE ONSET OF World War II set the stage for enormous changes in Florida. The state still lacked the factories and the labor force to play an important role in the direct war effort. Once again, however, the state's climate and geography—its great number of clear sunny days and relatively level terrain—made it a favorable location for training airmen. About 25 percent of the officers and 20 percent of the enlisted men who served in the Army Air Force were trained in the greater Miami Beach area alone. There was a large naval air station in Jacksonville and a Navy pilot training program at Pensacola; Dale Mabry Field in Tallahassee was a specialized base for pilots training to fly P-38s; and personnel were trained in amphibious warfare at Camp Gordon Johnston near Carrabelle. A large number of servicemen spent time in Florida and after the war many of them returned with families and friends to become permanent residents.

Florida agriculture contributed to the war effort: fresh vegetables were canned for military purposes, Florida beef became increasingly important, and canned orange juice and grapefruit sections were used in C-rations. Sugar was also important; it was the first food item to be rationed during the war, so its production in Florida got a new boost. But citrus production got the main boost. The technology of processing frozen juice concentrate, based on the technique used during the war to freeze-dry and concentrate blood and then to add water to it when and where it was needed, was an enormous boon to the industry, helping it to flourish after the war ended.

Tourism was sharply curtailed during the war, since gasoline rationing started soon after the United States entered the war and so much travel into Florida depended on the automobile. As early as the summer of 1943, however, tourists began coming back to Florida. Military training was completed by then, and many of the hotels used to house servicemen were returned to private control. Faced with the need to bring civilian tourists back into the state, local and state Chambers of Commerce began massive advertising campaigns encouraging people to come to Florida, and the legislature appropriated $1 million to advertise for tourists. Thus the period ended with the start of yet another growth spurt for Florida.

◆   ◆   ◆

During the war years Florida's women had a decreased interest in leisure handwork. Many women who had never worked away from their homes entered the work force full-time to replace men who were in military service. Women who had free time available devoted it to working for various civil defense or war-effort activities. This trend was evident in the small number of 1940s quilts registered by the Florida Quilt Heritage. A shortage of fabric during the war years meant that most of the quilts made were pieced scrap quilts fashioned from cloth already on hand.

A 1940s scrap quilt representing two generations of a family is the Wagon Wheel quilt owned by Mirtie Rhoden Crews and her husband, Raiford D. Crews (Plate 79). Large blocks made from printed feedsacks form the quilt backing. Mirtie's mother, Sydney Hayes Crews, pieced the top in the 1930s, and Mirtie did the quilting in the late 1940s.

Sydney was born in 1868 in Cobbtown, Georgia, married a farmer, Edward Asbury Crews, in 1886, and lived in southeastern Georgia and northeastern Florida. In her early teens she learned to quilt from her mother, using scraps left from making clothes, printed sugar, flour, and feed sacks, and fabrics purchased from dry goods stores. Their patterns and designs were handed down in the family from one generation to the next. Sydney made quilts for practical use by the family, and she also made coffin linings for the homemade caskets used at that time. Family members say that she kept the bereaved families occupied with interesting stories while the men made the casket and she worked on the fabric lining.

Sydney's daughter, Mirtie Rhoden Crews, was born in Baker County, Florida, in 1911. She also learned to quilt early in life, having older sisters to instruct her. Mirtie married Raiford D. Crews, a minister, in 1929, and they raised five children. She lived in Taylor, Jacksonville, and Sanderson, Florida. She quilted most of her years in her home and now quilts in the Sanderson Senior Center. She also spends time reading, crocheting, embroidering, and preserving and freezing fruits and vegetables for family enjoyment.

Bernice Partridge Oliver, Palm Bay, Florida, is the owner of a bold Double T scrap quilt that uses solids, woven plaids, and printed cottons in both the quilt top and its pieced backing (Plate 80). It was made for her by

PLATE 79. *Wagon Wheel.*
Made by Mirtie and Sydney
Hayes Crews in the late 1940s
in Baker County, Florida.
Dimensions, 67" × 84"; cot-
ton top; pieced by machine;
quilted by hand in fan pattern;
cotton batting; backing of cotton
print feedsacks.

her friends, Jessie Powell and Mrs. Masters, in 1941 as a wedding gift. Jessie was a retired nurse who was born in Quincy, Florida. She pieced the quilt and Mrs. Masters quilted it.

Since new fabrics were difficult to obtain during the war years, Margaret Bradley Hewett of Grand Ridge, Florida, was one of those quilters who reached into their scrap bags for materials. In the early 1940s she made the Fan Basket quilt in Plate 81, and still owns it today. Margaret was born in 1916 in Grand Ridge. She made this quilt top at the home of her father, before she married Robert James Hewett, a farmer and insurance salesman, in 1944. Her cousin Jessie Cook did the quilting. Margaret was an elementary school teacher in Jackson County, Florida, for thirty-six years, retiring in 1974. Since her retirement, Margaret has learned to do the quilting as well as the piecing of her quilts. She has made quilts for many family members and is now making one for each great-grandchild. She also works with a group of friends at the Grand Ridge Senior Center to make quilts for the needy in their community.

Linda Berke, Jacksonville, Florida, owns two scrap quilts made by her grandmother Etta Brownlee Raulerson and her great-aunt Ella Brownlee Varnes, a Grandmother's Fan quilt made in the 1930s or 1940s (Plate 82) and a beautifully organized one-patch Diamond Mine quilt made in the early 1940s (Plate 83). Both were made in Seville, Florida. The twin sisters who made them were born in Florida in the late 1800s into a pioneer family. Both became farmers' wives; Etta had five children and Ella, one. The quilts that they made were used as bedding for their families.

Another two-generation family quilt, the Mohawk Trail quilt in Plate 84 is owned by Wilma Friedel Ward, Evinston, Florida. It was pieced by Sarah Ethel Hunter Thayer, Wilma's grandmother, in Ohio, and was quilted in Florida by Wilma's mother, Selma Nettie Thayer Friedel, in 1943. Family members still have the cardboard templates used to cut the pieces for this quilt.

Sarah Ethel Hunter Thayer (1876–1942), born in Neoga, Illinois, learned to quilt at an early age, taught by her mother. In 1898 Sarah married Albert Ernest Thayer, who was in the insurance business, and lived most of her life in Illinois and Ohio. Sarah and her sisters exchanged letters about their quilts, shared patterns, and gave each other advice about setting blocks.

Sarah's daughter, Selma Nettie Thayer Friedel, was born in Neoga, Illinois, in 1900. She learned to quilt from her mother and aunts at an early age, often using family patterns and continuing the family tradition of sharing a family scrap bag along with some purchased materials. In 1923 she married William Charles Friedel. She quilted in her home, first in Cleveland, Ohio, later in Gainesville, Florida, and always kept a box of

PLATE 81. *Fan Basket. Pieced
by Margaret B. Hewett and
quilted by Jessie Cook in Grand
Ridge, Florida, in the early
1940s. Dimensions, 63½″ ×
74″; cotton top; pieced by hand
and machine; hand-quilted; cotton batting; blue cotton backing.*

Margaret B. Hewett.

PLATE 82. *Grandmother's Fan. Made by Etta Brownlee Raulerson and Ella Brownlee Varnes in Seville, Florida, in the 1930s and '40s. Dimensions, 69½" × 73"; cotton top; pieced by hand and machine; hand-quilted in outline pattern; cotton batting; plaid cotton backing.*

Ella Brownlee Varnes (left) and Etta Brownlee Raulerson (right).

PLATE 83. *Diamond Mine.*
Made by Etta Brownlee
Raulerson and Ella Brownlee
Varnes in the early 1940s in
Seville, Florida. Dimensions,

74" × 86½"; multicolor cotton
top; pieced by hand; hand-
quilted in all-over fan pattern;
cotton batting; plaid cotton
backing.

PLATE 84. *Mohawk Trail.*
Pieced by Sarah Ethel Thayer
in Ohio and quilted by Selma
Nettie Thayer Friedel in Gaines-
ville, Florida, in 1943. Di-
mensions, 81" × 87"; cotton
top; pieced by hand; fine hand-
quilting in clamshell and fan
designs; cotton batting; pink
cotton backing.

Sarah Ethel Hunter
Thayer (left). Selma
Nettie Thayer
Friedel (middle) and
her cousin Christine
Dugan (right).

Mattiewood Boney Staffiles in front of the family motel in High Springs, Florida.

cut pieces handy. Selma's children and grandchildren each have a prized quilt of her making.

The "Presidents" quilt in Plate 85 reflects the strong patriotism engendered by World War II and also provides evidence of the difficulty in obtaining high-quality fabrics during the war years. It was made by Mattiewood Boney Staffiles in High Springs, Alachua County, Florida, in 1945. Mattiewood was born in High Springs in 1927. Both she and her husband are retired schoolteachers and have three children; they now live in Oneco, Florida.

Mattiewood grew up in High Springs with her sister and two brothers. Both her parents were strict disciplinarians and always expected the children to do their share of family chores. At age five Mattiewood had already made a shirt on the sewing machine (with hand-worked buttonholes) that her father regularly wore to work as a locomotive engineer. When the family decided to build a motel in 1941, the children worked together to make hundreds of cement blocks for their father to use in construction. They mixed the mortar and packed the mixture into the forms to dry. Each child was paid a nickel for every block "made square and with no cracks."

While Mattiewood's mother helped her make her first quilt, she made the "Presidents" quilt by herself when she was in high school. She drew the pictures of the U.S. presidents, embroidered the outlines, assembled the top, and did the quilting. Mrs. Boney and the children shared all the motel duties, and Mattiewood spent many hours working on her quilt as she tended the office after school. Mattiewood had difficulty finding the solid red and blue that she needed for the quilt's patriotic theme. She purchased the only fabrics she could locate and discovered later that the colors had faded badly. She used the quilt in her dormitory room when at the Florida State College for Women in 1946.

PLATE 85. *"Presidents."*
Made by Mattiewood Bone
Staffiles in High Springs,
[Flor]ida, in 1945. Dimensions,
[ ] × 106"; cotton top; hand-
embroidered; hand-quilted
[in] parallel lines; cotton batti[ng];
cotton muslin backing.

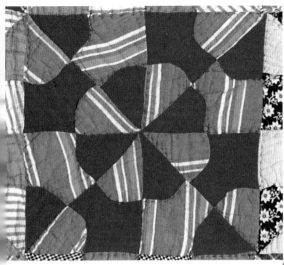

Post–World War II
to the Space Age
(1946–1975)

WORLD WAR II seemed to revitalize Florida. Highway and air transportation had accelerated so much during the war that, once the conflict ended in 1945, Florida had a transportation network ready for an endless caravan of new residents. Large numbers of veterans returned to Florida or moved into the state for the first time. Population growth in the next few decades exceeded wildest expectations.

When World War II ended, civilian concerns had been neglected for several years because of the war effort and shortages of materials. Millard Caldwell, who became Florida's governor in 1945, had the good fortune to inherit a surplus of about $8 million in state funds. Under his leadership the legislature added to the surplus, and Florida undertook a $30 million building program which included a Supreme Court building and various buildings at the three major state universities. The GI Bill was a great boon to higher education in Florida since so many returning veterans wanted the opportunity for an education. Both the University of Florida and the Florida State College for Women became coeducational schools, and the latter was renamed Florida State University.

Fuller Warren, following Caldwell in the governorship, faced a much more difficult challenge in terms of the state's finances. The surplus had been spent, and the rural-dominated legislature was lagging in raising revenue for the problems of South Florida. A limited 3 percent sales tax was passed, and there was some road construction.

Florida seemed to leap forward in several areas of governmental concern when LeRoy Collins became governor in 1955. Strongly aware of the need for Florida to have some type of economic development beyond tourism, Collins was the force behind the creation of the Florida Development Commission to attract capital, industry, and development to the state. His outlook on such issues as education, prisons, and increased funds for teachers' salaries was a progressive one. His efforts to make higher education available to all Floridians within thirty miles of their homes led to the development of Florida's community college system.

In the 1960s a conservative trend promoted growth in the ranks of the Republican party in Florida, particularly in West Florida and in the St. Petersburg-Tampa-Clearwater area, and the trend was reinforced as more people moved in from the North and some old-line Democrats switched parties. In 1962 the legislature increased the sales tax. Although integration was still token, blacks were beginning to attend Florida's public schools. The Florida Turnpike was extended from Ft. Pierce to Wildwood, giving tourism a major boost. A State Board of Regents was created to replace the Board of Control in exercising leadership of the state university system. Plans were made to expand the community college system and to create additional state universities.

In 1966, Claude Kirk was elected governor—the first Republican elected to the office since Reconstruction in 1872. In 1968, Ed Gurney, also a Republican, defeated LeRoy Collins in a race for a U.S. Senate seat. A new state constitution implemented reapportionment changes in 1968 along with other amendments involving terms for governors and the creation of the office of lieutenant governor. Florida retained its unique elected cabinet, although some of its functions were redistributed.

In the decades since World War II, Florida's economy has continued to diversify. Tourism, cattle, citrus, forest products, and phosphate remain important, but now they coexist with new industries that have expanded the jobs available to Floridians: space exploration, electronics, plastics, construction, real estate, and international banking.

The most significant trends of the postwar era have been steady population growth and desegregation. The state has also experienced a large migration of Cubans fleeing the Castro regime since the 1960s, the move to Florida of major American corporations in increasing numbers, completion of the interstate highway system throughout the state, construction of major international airports, expansion of the state's university and community college systems, mushrooming of suburban housing, introduction and expansion of high technology, and successful development of the NASA space program, highlighted by lunar landings, the space shuttle, and other historic launches from Cape Canaveral. Tourism is thriving as never before. Symbolic of the trend toward increasing sophistication in the tourism industry, Walt Disney World and its affiliated EPCOT Center have annually attracted more visitors from across the country and around the world than Florida has residents.

The women who entered the work force during World War II started a trend that has continued, and their numbers are ever increasing. As

Wilma Friedel Ward.

PLATE 86 *(opposite). "Powder Puff." Made by Wilma Friedel Ward in Gainesville, Florida, in 1949. Dimensions, 60" × 75"; top of cotton yo-yos; sewn by hand.*

in times past in Florida, a larger percentage of black women than white women are employed away from the home, but for both, most jobs are below the managerial level and are concentrated in areas historically considered most "acceptable" for women: teaching, nursing, clerical and secretarial, and fields related to home economics.

◆　　　　　　　◆　　　　　　　◆

Despite more labor-saving devices and freedom from the war effort, fewer women had an interest in quilting after the mid-1940s. Interesting technological changes occurred in sewing equipment and notions and the development of nylon and polyester led to new types and textures of fabrics. Some quilters experimented with the newer fabrics, but most of them returned to the use of all-cotton fabrics.

Wilma Friedel Ward owns a coverlet that she made in Gainesville, Florida, in 1949 and calls her "Powder Puff" quilt (Plate 86). It is made of 2,000 yo-yos, circular pieces of fabric that are gathered into puffs, flattened, and attached to each other with a few connecting stitches. Yo-yos were a popular method of using fabric remnants to make a coverlet that had a definite quilt look but was not actually quilted. Usually a yo-yo coverlet was sewn onto a solid color fabric backing or used over a colored bedspread. This coverlet is unusual in that it has been so carefully planned; most are assembled randomly. Its dark green solid fabric was purchased, but all the prints are from Wilma's three-generation family scrap collection.

Wilma was born in Cleveland, Ohio, in 1931, and learned to quilt at age eight or nine from her mother and grandmother. Wilma designs some of her quilt patterns, but often uses traditional patterns passed on by other family quilters. She married John Campray Ward in 1949, and now lives

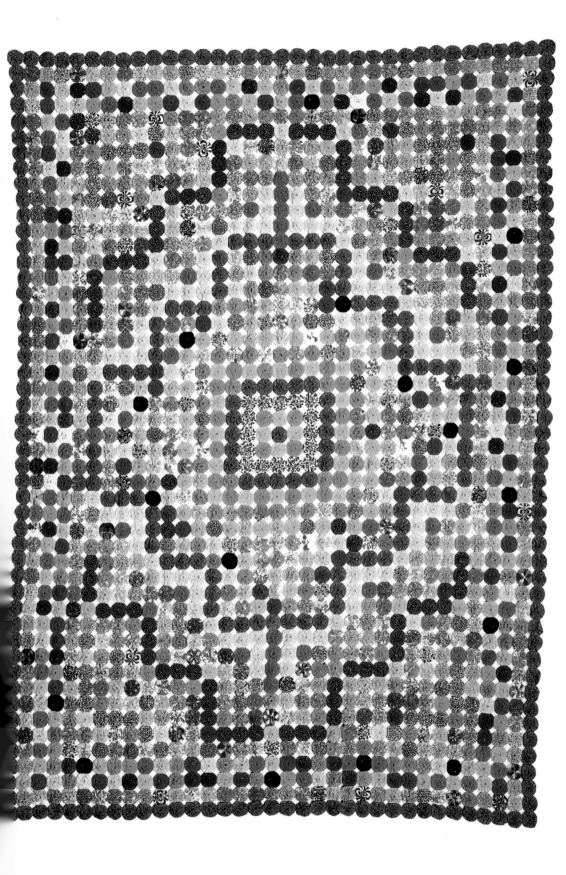

in Evinston, Florida. She quilts in her home almost every day, has made a quilt for each of her four children, and is currently working on completing one for each of her six grandchildren. Wilma's most prized possessions are three quilts—one made by her grandmother, one by her mother, and one that she made—that include pieces from identical fabrics.

Gloria C. Smith, Evinston, Florida, owns a Friendship Circle quilt (Plate 87) that was made by her grandmother Minnie Louise Thomas Gnann (1883–1969), in Gainesville, Florida, in 1950. Minnie was born in Clay County, Florida, and was only about seven years old when she learned to quilt from her mother and grandmother. In 1902 she married Eugene Gnann, who was in the lumber business, and lived at Penny Farms in Gainesville. She quilted daily and made many quilts. She presented this quilt to Gloria in 1954 as a wedding gift.

A quilt in the Hearts and Gizzards pattern (Plate 88) was given to its owner, Norma Johnson of Pensacola, Florida, by her grandmother Mary Etta Godwin. It was made in Pensacola in the mid-1950s. Mary Etta was born in 1895 at Marianna, Florida, and learned to quilt from her mother. Her frame was set up over the dining room table, and anyone who came to visit could join in the quilting. She used primarily scraps and feed sacks. Mary Etta made enough quilts for all her grandchildren; one Christmas she wrapped them as gifts with no name tags attached, and each grandchild picked a quilt sight unseen.

Mary E. Finley of Macclenny, Florida, assisted in supervising the construction of a Grandmother's Fan scrap quilt (Plate 89) that was made by the members of the Future Homemakers of America chapter at Baker County High School in 1957. When the quilt was raffled as a fund-raising project, Mary was the fortunate winner.

Georgia Myers Kenworthy of Miami, Florida, owns the "Peacock" quilt she made from her own design (Plate 90). She worked on the quilt in Iowa, Louisiana, and Texas for twenty-four years, from 1934 to 1958. Georgia was born in 1917 in Prairie City, Iowa, and learned to quilt when she was in her early teens from her mother. Her other interests are sewing, cooking, gardening, and arts and crafts, and she is an expert sheetrock hanger after helping her husband build a house from the ground up. She worked as a seamstress while her husband was attending law school and has also been employed as a bookkeeper and an office assistant.

When Georgia was sixteen, she completed the peacock design in a high school typing class. Her project of construction paper and colored typewriter ribbons was chosen by the teacher as one of the most complex and original. When Georgia announced that she wanted to make a one-of-a-kind quilt from her design, her mother told her to figure out the yardage needed and she would purchase the fabric for the project. Georgia's mother

PLATE 87. *Friendship Circle. Made by Minnie Louise Thomas Gnann in Gainesville, Florida, in 1950. Dimensions, 65" × 79"; cotton top; pieced by hand; quilted by hand in all-over pattern; cotton batting; pink cotton backing.*

Minnie Louise Thomas Gnann and her children.

PLATE 88. *Hearts and Gizzards. Made by Mary Etta Godwin in Pensacola, Florida, in the mid-1950s. Dimensions, 69" × 76"; top of cotton and cotton blend fabrics; pieced by hand; quilted by hand in outline pattern; cotton batting; red cotton backing.*

Mary Etta Godwin and her children.

PLATE 89. *Grandmother's Fan. Made in 1957 by members of the Future Homemakers of America chapter at Baker County High School in Macclenny, Florida. Dimensions, 75" × 95½"; top of cotton and cotton blend fabrics; piecing by hand and machine; hand-quilted in fan pattern; cotton batting; blue cotton backing.*

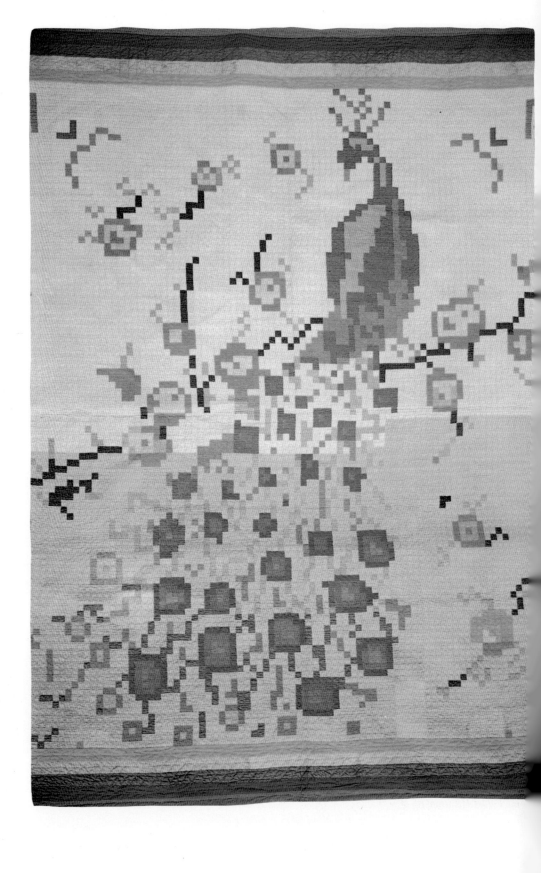

PLATE 90. *"Peacock." Pieced in 1958 by Georgia Myers Kenworthy of Miami, Florida. Dimensions, 88" × 100"; cotton top; pieced by machine; quilted by hand in diagonal grid; cotton batting; yellow cotton backing. Photo by Lane R. Kenworthy, Cutler Ridge, Florida.*

Georgia Myers Kenworthy.

was a perfectionist in her own needlework and suggested that Georgia pull threads for cutting each three-quarter-inch block so that they would be perfectly even. This was a very tedious and time-consuming procedure, but Georgia did it to make her mother proud of the result. All of the 9,064 tiny squares were carefully cut out and then pieced according to the intricate chart she had designed.

After many years of working on her traveling quilt project, Georgia completed the top in 1958, and a friend of her mother in Colfax, Iowa, did the quilting. Georgia moved to Florida in 1960. To her delight there are beautiful peacocks roaming freely around the Dade County neighborhood where she now lives, so she is surrounded by the beauty that inspired her design so many years age.

Dorothy Bellamy Robinson of Tallahassee, Florida, owns an unusual quilt that depicts figures and witty paraphrases from Greek mythology (Plate 91). It was appliquéd by her father, Dr. Raymond Bellamy, in Tallahassee in the 1960s. Raymond Bellamy was born in Moore's Hill, Indiana, married Laura Brooks in 1911, and was a professor and head of the Department of Sociology and Anthropology at the Florida State College for Women, later Florida State University, in Tallahassee. He also worked with the Boy Scouts of America, receiving their Silver Beaver Award in recognition of his efforts. His other interests were anthropological fieldwork, bird watching, cooking, gardening, FSU sports, writing—poetry and children's stories for his grandchildren, and scholarly articles in his academic fields—and making walking sticks (he donated his collection of about 400 wooden walking sticks he had made, each from a different native wood growing in Florida, to the Botany Department at FSU).

PLATE 91. *Greek mythology
quilt. Appliquéd by Raymond
Bellamy and quilted by a group
of Tallahassee women in the
1960s. Dimensions, 75½″ ×
83″; top of cotton and cotton
blend fabrics; appliquéd and
embroidered by hand; cotton
backing.*

Dr. Raymond Bellamy.

After Raymond's retirement from the university, he had to stay home a great deal because of his wife's failing health, and he took up appliqué as a means of passing the time. "Everybody in town" saved their pretty pieces of fabric for him, and he created eleven original appliquéd quilt tops. Various groups of women in Tallahassee helped with assembling and quilting.

An unusual manner of piecing the traditional Wedding Ring pattern resulted in a quilt pattern variation called Indian Wedding Ring (Plate 92), owned by Jane Thomas of Grand Ridge, Florida, and made by her great-aunt Phoebe Walsh in Gadsden County, Florida, in 1960. Phoebe was born in 1899 in Jackson County, Florida, and learned to quilt from her mother. She used a quilting frame and liked to work on her front porch in warm weather and inside by the fireplace on cooler days.

Lyma Raulerson, Macclenny, Florida, is the owner of a Dutch Rose quilt (Plate 93) made by Alma Knabb Raulerson (1894–1974), mother of Lyma's husband, T. J. Raulerson, in Macclenny about 1960. Alma was born in the Taylor section of Baker County, the youngest of three children of Sarah Brown and Thomas Jefferson Knabb. In 1911 she married George Raulerson, and for years the couple operated a general store in the building that now houses the Senior Center in downtown Macclenny. Alma made numerous quilts for her family and in her later years she sold a few.

A seldom-seen quilt pattern called Pine Cone is shown in Plate 94. It is owned by Willie J. Hutchison of Marianna, Florida, and was made in Marianna in 1966 by Addie Bullock (1897–1967), a friend of Willie's mother. The Pine Cone pattern is formed by stitching folded points in concentric circles, resulting in a heavy quilt with ten or more thicknesses of fabric in some sections.

Addie Bullock was born in Sneads, Florida, and learned to quilt at age twelve from her sister. They used cotton and wool scraps from family and friends to make bedding for the family. Addie married George Bullock and the couple raised eighteen children—twelve of their own and six foster children. She found time to garden and sew and quilted when she could fit it into her busy days.

Frances Boone Thomson (1865–1971) made a taffeta Rolling Star quilt (Plate 95) in St. Petersburg, Florida, in 1967 that is now owned by her daughter, H. Berniece Thompson of Gulfport, Florida. Frances was born in Agency, Missouri, and learned to quilt in her preteen years from her mother. She married a pharmacist, and they raised three children. Frances was always interested in sewing and earned income as a seamstress, but not as a quilter. She quilted in her home in St. Petersburg, using both taffeta and cotton fabrics that she purchased especially for her quilt making. She preferred to use a hoop rather than a frame.

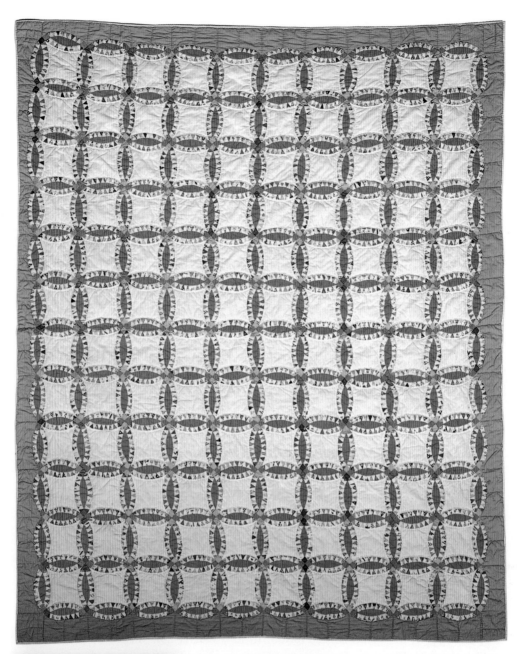

PLATE 92. *Indian Wedding Ring. Made by Phoebe Walsh in Gadsden County, Florida, in 1960. Dimensions, 68" × 85½"; cotton top; pieced by hand; fine hand-quilting; cotton batting; yellow cotton backing.*

Phoebe Walsh.

PLATE 93. *Dutch Rose. Made by Alma Knabb Raulerson in Macclenny, Florida, about 1960. Dimensions, 69" × 84"; cotton top; pieced by hand; quilted by hand; cotton batting; blue-grey cotton backing.*

Alma Knabb Raulerson.

PLATE 94. *Pine Cone. Made
by Addie Bullock in Marianna,
Florida, in 1966. Dimensions,*
*63" × 86"; cotton top; sewn by
hand; quilted by hand; no batting; striped cotton backing.*

PLATE 95. *Rolling Star. Made by Frances Boone Thomson in St. Petersburg, Florida, in 1967. Dimensions, 85" × 107"; taffeta top; pieced by hand and machine; hand-quilted in crosshatch and parallel patterns; blanket used as batting; white cotton backing.*

Frances Boone Thomson.

PLATE 96. "Odd Fellow."
Made by Rose Woods in Ft.
Lauderdale, Florida, in 1968.
Dimensions, 65½" × 80";
cotton top; pieced by machine;
fine hand-quilting; polyester
batting; white cotton backing.

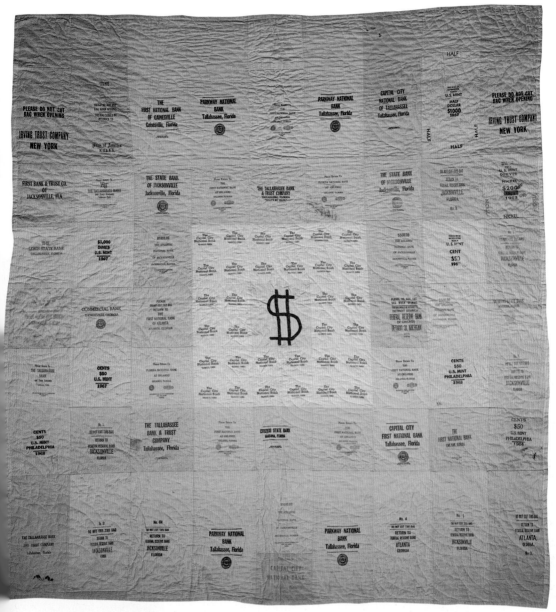

PLATE 97. *"Money Bags." Made by Sarah Elvie Whaley Durrance in Tallahassee, Florida, in 1969. Dimensions, 90 ½" × 98"; top constructed of natural cotton coin bags; pieced by hand and machine; quilted by hand in fan pattern; cotton batting; cotton muslin backing.*

Sarah Elvie Whaley Durrance.

"Odd Fellow" is the name of a charm quilt (Plate 96) owned by Rose Woods and made by her in 1968 in Ft. Lauderdale, Florida. A charm quilt is a special type of scrap quilt in which each patch is cut in the same shape but from a different piece of fabric. Often the patches are collected from the quilt maker's friends and relatives. This quilt contains a piece of fabric from the dress in which Rose's mother was baptized. She made the quilt while her husband was serving in Vietnam, and it was exhibited in a quilt show in Augsburg, Germany, in 1976.

Rose Woods was born in 1937 in Harman, Virginia, and lived in Virginia until she was fifteen years old. In 1956 she married James C. Woods, now an electronics technician retired from the U.S. Army. She spent twenty-three years as an Army wife, including ten years in Germany; they now live in Green Cove Springs, Florida. Rose learned to quilt at age thirty with some assistance from her mother. Her patterns were gleaned from family, friends, books, and magazines.

While living in Germany, Rose received a certificate of appreciation from the U.S. Army for participating in Germany's first quilt show and a quilting demonstration during the American Bicentennial celebration in 1976. She also organized a quilting bee and taught quilting classes in Germany from 1975 to 1977.

William J. Gladwin, Jr., of Tallahassee, Florida, owns a novelty quilt named "Money Bags" (Plate 97). Created by William's grandmother Sarah Elvie Whaley Durrance (1893–1983) in 1969 in Tallahassee, it is made of coin bags almost exclusively from Florida banks. William saved the coin bags when he was working as a teller at the Capital City First National Bank in Tallahassee, and his grandmother (with some assistance from William) made the quilt as a bedcover for him.

Sarah Elvie (Sallie) Whaley Durrance was born in Medart, Wakulla County, Florida, one of eight children in a pioneer farm family. She learned to quilt at about age twelve from her mother and quilted daily when she was in her twenties and thirties. She went to school in Medart and Lloyd, Florida, and in 1912 married Earlie Harris Durrance in Medart. They raised four children. He was a farmer, grist mill owner, and postmaster for Medart. Sallie was widowed in 1922 and, following secretarial training, began working at the Florida Motor Vehicle Commission in 1924. She retired in 1972 after a forty-eight-year career.

Bicentennial to
the Present
(1976–1988)

◆ ◆ ◆

THROUGHOUT THE LATE 1970s and the 1980s Florida continued to experience spectacular growth. In 1980 the state's population was approaching 10 million and by 1988 had grown to almost 12.5 million residents. Hundreds of new residents are added to this total every day, coming to Florida from all sections of the nation. Sizable numbers of black and Hispanic residents, important segments of the state's population, participate actively in Florida's economy, politics, and educational systems. Another ethnic group, the Seminole Indians, have increased to about 1,800, residing in seven reservations at Immokalee, Hollywood, and Brighton and along the Big Cypress Swamp. The Seminoles continue to be survivors in a difficult environment. In addition to cattle raising, craft sales, tobacco shops, and a hotel in Tampa, the Seminole tribe operates a profitable bingo parlor, and they have become financially independent.

The state's economy is still based largely on its geography and climate, and today Florida's most important industries include tourism, agriculture, phosphate mining, forest products, and aerospace enterprises. A budding motion picture industry is also getting under way in the Orlando area.

Bob Graham, Florida's two-term Democratic governor from 1979 to 1987, provided effective leadership for the state in such critical times as the Cuban-Haitian influx of 1980 and, in the same year, civil disturbances in the Miami area. Graham helped to push programs through the legislature to deal with environmental priorities such as saving the rivers, coastal areas, and Everglades and restoring and protecting Florida's water supply (Morris, pp. 336–37). During the late 1980s the state again took a strong conservative turn, electing Bob Martinez, a Republican, as governor in 1987.

Special problems facing Florida's leaders and people in the 1990s are growth management, protection of the state's fragile environment, the drug war, and the increasing violence facing Floridians in their everyday lives.

Well over half of Florida's women are now working outside their homes, putting in forty or more hours at work, plus commuting time, and up to thirty-five hours of housework each week. Life for most people of all ages and both sexes can be hectic and stressful, and the influence of many scientific and technological advances that affect the life of each person is not always benevolent. This life-style seems to have led to a renewed need for the personalized and the natural aspects of life.

During the years just preceding the U.S. Bicentennial, a remarkable resurgence of interest in quilt making began. The catalyst was a 1971 show at the Whitney Museum of American Art in New York City, entitled "Abstract Design in American Quilts." Its success had an amazing effect. People began buying quilts as never before. Quilt collections grew rapidly; quilters' organizations formed; quilt shops opened, offering a wide array of classes to aspiring quilters as well as providing specialized fabrics and notions; the publication of magazines and newsletters aimed at quilters got under way; and quilt shows sprang up all across the nation. With the renaissance of quilt making, many of the old traditions were reappearing—quilting bees, friendship quilts, making quilts for fund raising, and the creating of group quilts to commemorate special family, community, or historical events (Wilder, p. 196).

Another milestone in modern quilting was the 1976 Great American Quilt Contest, inspired by the Bicentennial celebration and sponsored by *Good Housekeeping* magazine, the United States Historical Society, and New York's Museum of American Folk Art. There were nearly 10,000 entries and a first prize of $2,500 (Wilder, p. 196). Before 1979 most exhibitions featured quilts executed in traditional patterns, techniques, and colors, and there were few opportunities available to artists who worked with original designs, materials, and techniques. The annual Quilt National shows in Athens, Ohio, promote interest in quilts as a contemporary art form and have featured some of the most innovative designs being produced (Wilder, p. 197). The most spectacular quilting event held to this date was the Great American Quilt Festival in New York City in April 1986. This event was organized by the Museum of American Folk Art to celebrate the Statue of Liberty Centennial. Widespread promotional activities and the participation of tens of thousands of quilters in this event did much to put quilting back into the hearts, heads, and hands of millions of Americans (Wilder, p. 197).

As a result of expanding interest in quilts and quilt collecting, many states have become aware of the need to document and record important historical information about their quilts. Through the combined efforts of concerned quilters and historians, studies such as the Florida Quilt Heritage Project are being completed in many areas of the country.

The effect of the quilting renaissance is obvious in the large numbers and great variety of contemporary quilts that were discovered and registered in Florida during the project. All the quilts selected for inclusion in this book from the period 1976–88 were made in Florida. Of these thirty-nine quilts, twenty-five are original designs and fourteen use traditional patterns in unusual or original arrangements or combinations. Another aspect of quilting that has changed is that most of these quilts were made for decorative or commemorative purposes rather than for use as bed coverings.

For a Bicentennial commemorative quilt made in 1976 (Plate 98), members of Florida Extension Homemakers clubs all over the state made blocks, and forty were chosen as county winners. The quilt was made in cooperation with the Gainesville Quilting Association. Its members assembled the winning blocks and did the quilting. The finished quilt was shared with over 300,000 viewers at fifty locations around the state before it was donated to the collection of the Museum of Florida History in 1978.

The blocks representing Florida counties and their creators were: Hillsborough, Alice G. Cash (Ruskin); Pinellas, Mrs. Glenn Seman (Treasure Island); Okaloosa, Bertha Mae Corkins (Crestview); Alachua, Irene Ford (Melrose); Dade, Mrs. Kenneth Berghuis, Sr. (Miami); Columbia, Mabel Wolford (Lake City); Hamilton, F. Vocke; Volusia, Mrs. V. G. Baldwin, Sr. (Oak Hill); Marion, Edith Williams (Ocala); Putnam, Hazel Hand (Palatka); Franklin, Martha F. Fritz (Carrabelle); St. Johns, Carol Neuenfeldt (St. Augustine); Lee, Marjorie Soto (Ft. Myers); Suwannee, Mrs. Willie Haas; Holmes, Tennie Collins; Jackson, Mrs. Wayne DeWitt; Levy, Betty Parker (Williston); Leon, Nona Sherill; Lake, Helen VanAuken (Paisley); Seminole, Ellarea Broderick (Altamonte Springs); Polk, Anice Bellinger (Lakeland); Walton, Mary Leonard (DeFuniak Springs); Orange, Mary Davis (Union Park) and Barbara Weber (Orlando); Clay, Lucille Nichols and Thelma Kirkland (Green Cove Springs); Escambia, Alma Watson (Cantonment); Osceola, Laura Miller (Kissimmee); Highlands, Ruby Mielke (Lake Placid); Duval, Tina Griffin; Citrus, Elsie Knapp (Inverness); Nassau, Lynda Petree (Callahan); Santa Rosa, Lorena Rife (Milton); Pasco, Ida Mae Bechtel (Port Richey); Manatee, Florence Heeren (Oneco); Hardee, Pearl Hendry; Collier, Georgia

PLATE 98. *Bicentennial com-* *memorative quilt. Made by* *Florida Extension Homemakers* *Clubs of Florida in 1976; now* *part of the collection of the* *Museum of Florida History,* *Tallahassee. Dimensions, 75"* *× 87½"; top of polyester-cotton* *blends; pieced and appliquéd* *by hand and machine;hand-* *embroidered; hand-quilted;* *polyester batting; cotton backing.*

Horton (Bonita Springs); Brevard, South Tropical Homemakers Club; Sumter, Shirley Fox; Flagler, Louella Fleurie (Flagler Beach); Desoto, Dorothy Buchfinck (Arcadia); Palm Beach, Florence Michielangelo (West Palm Beach); Wakulla, Doris Harrison (Sopchoppy); and the Extension Seal block, Alice G. Cash (Ruskin).

A brilliant Star of Bethlehem quilt, another tribute to the Bicentennial (Plate 99), is owned by Linda G. McCollum of McIntosh, Florida, and was made in McIntosh by her mother, Audrey Waters Cannon, in 1976. Audrey was born in 1921 in Bell, Florida, Gilchrist County, a third-generation Floridian. She pieced her first quilt top at age eleven and learned how to quilt, after she married Woodrow Wilson Cannon, from her mother-in-law, Maude Cannon. Woodrow was a farmer, and at one time the couple worked together as cottage parents for Sunland Training Center, an institution for handicapped children. The Cannons raised three children, and Audrey was a role model of strength and independence as they were growing up. At first she made quilts as bedding for family use; however, as her skill and involvement grew, the creation of quilts became a means of artistic expression. During some periods of difficulty in her life, Audrey found solace in her stitchery, and she says her quilt making became her means of creating "beauty from ashes."

Mable Scofield Wolford, Lake City, Florida, is the designer, maker, and owner of a quilt named "Florida Forest" (Plate 100). Her design for the block unit of this quilt was chosen to represent Columbia County in a Bicentennial quilt that was a joint project of the Florida State Council of Extension Homemakers Clubs and the Gainesville Quilting Association. Her block design includes a pine tree, palmetto fronds, sky, and a representation of Ocean Pond, a pond near her home. Mable then entered the block in a national contest sponsored by *Progressive Farmer* magazine, and it was selected as one of the top ten entries. The block is featured, along with forty-nine other original designs, in the book *Prize Country Quilts,* by Mary Elizabeth Johnson. In 1979 Mable made the quilt pictured here, which repeats her original block as the design unit for the entire quilt.

Mable was born in 1922 in Lake City, Florida, where she lives today. She first became interested in quilting through watching her mother and grandmother, and she made her first quilt at age eighteen. She quilts nearly every day, often using a frame, but she also works with a hoop and does lap quilting as well. Mable is married and the mother of three children. Her quilts are made for practical use by her family, and she is making a quilt for each of her children.

Mable is part of a family that has been in Columbia County for more than a hundred years: "My life and that of my ancestors is inextricably entwined with the beautiful trees, palmettos and lakes of the Osceola Na-

PLATE 99. *Star of Bethlehem. Made by Audrey Waters Cannon in Gainesville, Florida, in 1976. Dimensions, 88" × 88"; cotton top; pieced by hand; quilted by hand in diamond grid pattern; polyester batting; cotton fabric backing. Photograph courtesy of Linda G. McCollum.*

Audrey Waters Cannon.

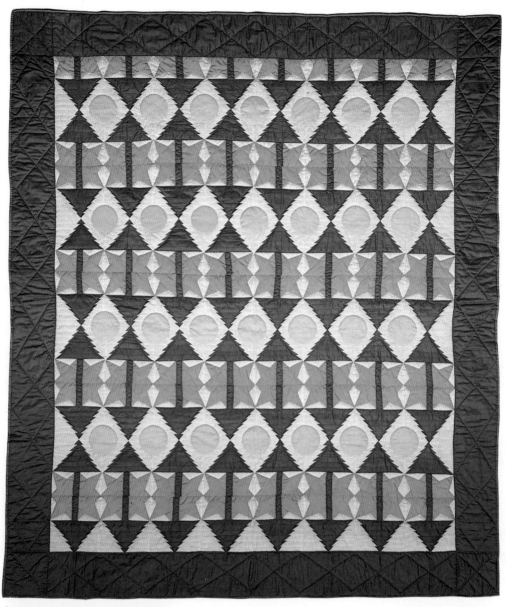

PLATE 100. *"Florida Forest."* *Designed and made by Mable Scofield Wolford in 1979 in Lake City, Florida. Dimensions, 86" × 96"; top of* *cotton-polyester blend; pieced by machine; quilted by hand; polyester batting; cotton-polyester blend backing.*

Mable Scofield Wolford and Kenneth Wolford.

tional Forest. . . . My great-grandfather came to Florida in 1853 and set-tled in this forest land where he married, built a home, and raised a family. He joined the Confederate Army in the second year of the Civil War. He belonged to Company E of the Ninth Florida regiment and was with Lee at Appomattox when he surrendered. In 1931, when the Osceola National Forest was established, my grandparents could not bear to give up their land to the government. They were allowed to keep their land and live inside the forest. Some of the land still belongs to the family, and I have an eighty-seven-year-old aunt living in the house that was built by my great-grandfather. The walls of my home are paneled with red heart cypress which my husband and my uncle dragged from the forest floor. . . . These logs were probably dead and downed before Columbus discovered Amer-ica. I have many wonderful memories of this forest land and this is what inspired me to make this quilt block."

The "Gunter Family History" quilt (Plate 101) is a commemorative quilt that depicts fifty years in the life of the Gunter family. The quilt, made by members of the family and their friends throughout the state, was pre-sented to Dawson and Tillie Gunter of Ocala, Florida, on their fiftieth wedding anniversary. The Gunters' daughter, Merilyn G. Atkins, initiated the project, supplying information and selecting colors. Her husband, Dick Atkins, a project engineer at the Orlando Naval Training Center, drew the patterns for the blocks on graph paper and Merilyn color-coded them. Embroidery work began after Thanksgiving in 1979, and the twenty pictorial blocks were then assembled into the quilt. The nineteen quilt makers are all Florida residents: Merilyn Atkins, Hattie Summer, Teresa Gunter, Natalie Senterfitt, Ruth Senterfitt, Margie Thurmond, Cristi Strange, Amy Atkins, Nancy Atkins, Ida Paul, Evelyn Horsley, Beverly Breshere, Mildred Hamlett, Margie Frank, Alisa Gunter, Odessa Goff, Frances Townsend, Alberta Irey, and Doris McLeod. More than 300 fam-ily members and friends shared the the Gunters' happiness and surprise when the quilt was presented to Dawson and Tillie at their golden wed-ding reception in Orlando on April 13, 1980.

A medallion-type quilt using the World without End pattern in the cen-ter surrounded by sections of the Whirlwind block (Plate 102) is owned by Wendy Elizabeth Whitaker of Orlando, Florida, and was made by her grandmother, Cathy Whitaker, in Orlando in 1980. Cathy grew up in western North Carolina, where making quilts was a part of everyday life. Her involvement with quilts can be traced back to the 1930s, when she was a young newspaper reporter in Asheville, North Carolina. She remembers being distressed when she discovered that handmade quilts were being used to protect the loads of tobacco that the farmers brought to the ware-house. After the tobacco had been carefully transferred to the warehouse

PLATE 101. *"Gunter Family History" quilt. Made by nineteen family members and friends throughout Florida in 1979–80. Dimensions, 78" × 94¾"; top of Aida fabric and cotton-polyester blend; pieced by hand and machine; hand-quilted in the border of each block; polyester batting; cotton-polyester blend backing.*

Teresa and Bill Gunter and their children.

PLATE 102. *World without*
End and Whirlwind. Made by
Cathy Whitaker in Orlando,
Florida, in 1980. Dimensions,
68" × 88½; cotton top; pieced
by machine; hand-quilted in
outline pattern; polyester bat-
ting; cotton-polyester blend
backing. Photograph courtesy
of Cathy Whitaker.

baskets, she would see the same quilts warming the farmers as they slept in their trucks, awaiting their payments from the sales.

In 1981 Julia Smallwood Wernicke of Pensacola, Florida, made a modern crazy quilt named "This Is Your Life" (Plate 103) for her daughter and son-in-law, Dale and Michael Edlebeck, also of Pensacola. It represents interests and events in the lives of the Edlebecks and includes motifs representing their hobbies (biking, swimming, aerobics, canoeing, and jogging), their academic degrees, important family dates, Dale's pets, and Mike's military career (helicopter and Marine wings), as well as assorted ribbons and bird and flower patches. The patches are embellished by twenty-eight different types of embroidery stitches. The quilt was presented to Dale and Michael for Christmas 1981.

Julia was born in 1918 in New Bern, North Carolina. She married Roger Moore Wernicke, and they have two children. Julia learned to quilt as an adult and is largely self-taught. "This Is Your Life" won the best-of-show award in the Gulf Coast Stitchery Guild show in 1982 and a first-place ribbon in its category at the National Quilting Association national show in 1982. Julia also made a crib quilt, Tulip Cross appliqué (Plate 104) in 1984, which she designed after an 1865 crib quilt.

"Cosmic Cotillion" (Plate 105) is a vibrantly colored quilt owned and made by Anna Lupkiewicz of Gainesville, Florida, in 1981. Anna was born in 1917 in Rochester, New York. After receiving a bachelor of fine arts degree in music, she completed a performer's degree in voice at the University of Rochester and married Joseph Lupkiewicz. The couple moved to Florida with their three children in 1949 when Joseph joined the music faculty at the University of Florida in Gainesville. He was the director of the Men's Glee Club at the university, and they both took part in many local musical productions.

Anna developed an admiration for quilts early in her life but never found anyone to teach her how to make a quilt until 1970, when she attended a senior citizens' quilting class and was "smitten." Now she quilts almost every day, teaches quilting at Santa Fe Community College, and participates in a great many workshops and demonstrations in the Gainesville area. Anna has sent some of her quilt work to be exhibited in Novorossiisk, Russia, Gainesville's sister city. She received a Florida State Folk Arts grant in 1983 to research black women and their quilts and had the honor of being named the Outstanding Senior Citizen of the Year in Gainesville in 1985.

Jacqueline Simoneaux of Jacksonville, Florida, is the owner of a Feathered Star quilt she made in Jacksonville in 1981 (Plate 106). Jackie was born in 1938 in Caribou, Maine, lived there until she was thirteen, and then spent seven years in New Jersey. In 1958 she married Jules Simoneaux

PLATE 103. *"This Is Your Life." Made by Julia Small-wood Wernicke in Pensacola, Florida, in 1981. Dimensions,* 32" × 40"; *top of various silk and polyester fabrics; pieced by hand and machine; hand-appliquéd and hand-embroidered;* brown cotton-polyester blend backing.

PLATE 104. *Tulip Cross appliqué. Made by Julia Smallwood Wernicke in Pensacola, Florida, in 1984. Dimensions, 42" × 42"; cotton top; appliquéd by hand; fine hand-quilting in outline and echo patterns; polyester batting; tan cotton backing.*

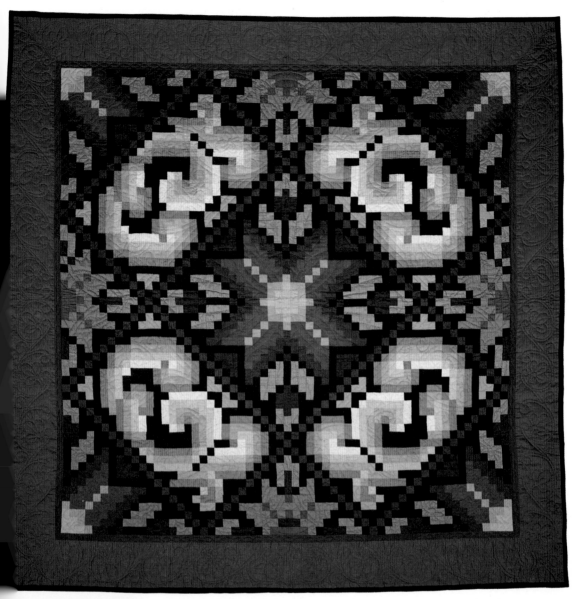

PLATE 105. *"Cosmic Cotillion." Made by Anna Lupkiewicz in 1981 in Gainesville, Florida. Dimensions, 92" × 92"; cotton top; pieced by machine; hand-quilted in circular floral design; polyester batting; cotton backing.*

Anna Lupkiewicz.

PLATE 106. *Feathered Star with Swag and Tassel border. Made by Jacqueline Simoneaux of Jacksonville, Florida, in 1981. Dimensions, 71½" × 71½"; cotton top; pieced and appliquéd by hand; hand-quilted in diamond, crosshatch, outline, and floral patterns; polyester batting; green cotton backing.*

(now retired from the U.S. Navy), spent fourteen years traveling as a Navy wife, and has lived for the past seventeen years in Jacksonville. She received a degree from Jacksonville University in mathematics and humanities with minors in computer science and physics and worked for the City of Jacksonville for three years as a systems analyst but found that she was not enjoying this work. Jackie is now a self-taught quilter who teaches classes and quilts in her studio at home for family members as well as on commission for others.

Jackie's "Butterflies" sampler wall quilt (Plate 107) was made in 1983 in Jacksonville. It won blue ribbons at the 1985 North Carolina Quilt Symposium and the 1985 National Quilting Association annual national show. Jackie explains her love of quilting: "Quilting satisfies my soul in ways that nothing else has ever done. It has order and design and color and intuitive use of fabrics. I am a very tactile person and the feel of the fabrics is part of what I enjoy about quilting. I enjoy the whole process—design, execution of design in fabric, quilting the project, and the look and feel of the finished quilt."

Stephanie Metts of Gainesville, Florida, is the owner and maker of a quilt constructed in the stained-glass technique and named "Rose Cathedral" (Plate 108). She made the quilt in 1981 in Gainesville. Stephanie was born in 1942 in Jacksonville, Florida. Her husband is a Certified Public Accountant and hospital administrator, and they have three children. She is a retired shop owner who learned to quilt on her own at age thirty-two and later took classes. She quilts at home, where she "looks out on Possum Creek," and uses a variety of fabrics, most of which are purchased especially for her quilting. This particular quilt depicts the window of the Cathedral Window Quilt Shoppe in Gainesville, which is patterned after windows in Chartres Cathedral in France.

A contemporary crazy-patch quilt called "Red Squares" (Plate 109) made in 1983 and a small wall quilt called "Fruit of the Bloom" made in 1984 (Plate 110) are owned by their maker, Dixie Haywood, of Pensacola, Florida. Dixie was born in 1933 in Seattle, Washington, and has lived in Washington, California, Oklahoma, and Florida. She is married and has three children. She is a self-taught quilter who quilts daily to weekly, depending on her travel schedule. Dixie has owned a quilt shop and has earned income from teaching quilting, designing quilts, writing about quilts, and making custom-ordered quilts. She developed a contemporary crazy-quilting technique and published *The Contemporary Crazy Quilt Project Book* in 1977 and *Crazy Quilting with a Difference* in 1981, the latter reprinted in 1986 as *Crazy Quilt Patchwork*.

Dixie worked on her "Fruit of the Bloom" quilt throughout a period when her husband was experiencing severe health problems, and the

PLATE 107. *"Butterflies."*
Made by Jacqueline Simoneaux,
Jacksonville, Florida, in 1983.
Dimensions, 28" × 42"; top of
cotton and cotton-polyester blend
fabrics; appliquéd by hand and
pieced by machine; fine hand-
quilting; polyester batting; blue
cotton backing.

Jacqueline Simoneaux.

PLATE 108. "Rose Cathedral." Made by Stephanie Metts in Gainesville, Florida, in 1981. Dimensions, 102" × 103"; top made in stained-glass tech-nique, of polished cotton fabric; hand-appliquéd; fine hand-quilting in outline, echo, and other patterns; polyester batting; red cotton backing.

PLATE 109. *"Red Squares."*
Made by Dixie Haywood of
Pensacola, Florida, in 1983.
Dimensions, 66" × 80"; cot-
ton top; pieced by machine;
hand-quilted in outline and
channel patterns; polyester bat-
ting; beige cotton backing.

PLATE 110. *"Fruit of the Bloom." Made by Dixie Haywood of Pensacola, Florida, in 1984. Dimensions, 44" × 52"; cotton top; pieced by machine; appliquéd by hand with a reverse appliqué border; fine hand-quilting in outline pattern; polyester batting; natural cotton backing.*

quilt's subject matter (the life cycle of a watermelon, one of his favorite foods) and beautifully executed design became symbolic to them of the cycle of their relationship.

Florida creatures are featured in a machine-quilted work called "Blue Domain" (Plate 111), made by Agnes Adams Adkison in Gulf Breeze, Florida, in 1983. Born in Cannon County, Tennessee, Agnes is a homemaker and teacher who has five children. She became acquainted with quilting at an early age but did not actually try it herself until she was about thirty. She says that she learned by observation, trial and error, and instruction in quilting classes. She quilts about four days a week at her home in Gulf Breeze.

"A Salute to Space Exploration," a quilt celebrating the first twenty-five years of the space age (Plate 112), is owned by George L. Giefer of Melbourne, Florida, and was made by his wife, Florence J. Giefer, in 1983, in Melbourne. Florence Jane Cochran Giefer was born in 1936 in Leewood, West Virginia. In 1961 she came to Florida, where she met and married George, and they have raised three children. Florence learned to quilt at an adult center in Melbourne in early 1983 and made the quilt for her husband for a Christmas surprise. George works for RCA at Cape Canaveral. Their son, George, Jr., and their daughter, Kathleen Vanderhoofven, both helped with the design and construction. The family had to work on the quilt only when George was not at home, which slowed their progress somewhat. The quilt tells the story of the first twenty-five years of NASA and of Americans exploring space, and it includes the names of all astronauts who have traveled in space through the end of the twenty-fifth year and a complete set of launch patches up to that time. Symbols of the United States have been used for some of the quilting designs around the border—eagles, stars, and shields.

An unusual quilted wall hanging made in 1984 is an example of the renewed interest in preserving and sharing family history. Owned by Patricia S. Buek of Melbourne Beach, Florida, the quilt is called the "Generations Quilt" (Plate 113). It was made in Florida by Patricia's daughter, Sharon Buek Houchens, and is one of a series of five quilts that feature reproductions of photographs, tintypes, and pen-and-ink sketches of family members. The focal point of the quilt is a photograph of four generations in the family—Sharon, her daughter, her mother, and her grandmother. On each side are pictures of grandparents, great-grandparents, and great-great-grandparents.

Sharon was born in Philadelphia, Pennsylvania, in 1948 and became a Florida resident in 1965. She graduated from Vero Beach High School and Florida Atlantic University and married Gary L. Houchens, an aerospace engineer, in 1970. They have two children and currently reside in Renton,

PLATE III. *"Blue Domain."*
Made by Agnes Adams Adkison
1983 in Gulf Breeze, Flor-
a. Dimensions, 41" × 58";
p of cotton-polyester blend

fabrics; pieced by machine;
machine-appliquéd; machine-
quilted in echo pattern; polyester
batting; cotton-polyester blend
backing.

PLATE 112. *"A Salute to Space Exploration." Designed and made by Florence Jane Cochran Giefer in Melbourne in 1983. Dimensions, 84" × 104½"; top of cotton-polyester blend fabrics; pieced by hand and machine; machine-appliquéd; hand-quilting includes patriotic symbols; polyester batting; white cotton-polyester blend backing.*

George L. and Florence Jane Cochran Giefer.

PLATE 113. *"Generations."
Made in Florida in 1984 by
Sharon Buek Houchens.
Dimensions, 44" × 44"; cotton top; appliquéd by hand;
hand-quilted in grid pattern;
polyester batting; burgundy cotton backing. Photo by David
Gatlin, Vero Beach, Florida.*

Sharon Buek Houchens.

Washington. Sharon had done handwork since she was in elementary school, but her interest in quilting was sparked by the wedding gift of a quilt from her new mother-in-law, and she began collecting fabric scraps for quilts she hoped to make someday. For the years that Gary was in the Air Force the couple moved around extensively, and while he was stationed at Newark, Ohio, a group of Methodist church women taught Sharon how to quilt. After many "fits and starts" she got her first quilt completed with their help; she now completes an average of one a year. For almost all of her work she uses cotton fabric, much of it from family, friends, and garage sales and some of it purchased. Since living on the West Coast, Sharon has been active in starting quilters' groups, giving quilting demonstrations in schools, and assisting with the organization of quilt shows. Her involvement with quilting is now an integral part of her life to the point that she says, "I always have a quilt in the frame, one ready to be put in the frame, one being hand-pieced, one cut out, one in my mind, and one on my bed! I love to quilt!"

Florence Renney of Brooksville, Florida, designed and coordinated the construction of a quilt made by twenty-two members of the Brooksville Woman's Club in 1984 (Plate 114). It has been exhibited at local Woman's Club meetings and at district and state meetings. The quilt features the Woman's Club building in the center, and all past presidents' names are embroidered on it.

Juliet Brown Blum's Rose Variation quilt (Plate 115) is a copy of a quilt her grandmother made over one hundred years ago (see Plate 25). Juliet made her quilt in Sarasota, Florida, in 1984. She was born in Akron, Ohio, in 1917, and married William George Blum, a salesman who is now retired, in 1936; they have five children and nine grandchildren. Juliet learned to quilt when she was thirty-five from her mother and now quilts every week, using some patterns handed down in her family and some new ones from books and magazines. She began with a crib quilt for a new grandson and, after making numerous others, started working on assembling the fabrics needed to carry out her dream of making a copy of the quilt that her grandmother, Emeline Hayward Brown, had made for her hope chest in the 1870s. Finding just the right prints took several years, and she began drafting her patterns and cutting out pieces in the summer of 1980 with the help of her daughter, Dr. Julia Blum. The quilt was completed and ready for display in 1985.

There is an old saying that once you get Florida sand in your shoes, you will return someday—most likely the inspiration for Aloyse Yorko of Bokeelia, Florida, to name her quilt "Sand in Our Shoes" (Plate 116). She made the quilt in 1984 in Jupiter, Florida. Aloyse was born in 1934 in Punxsutawney, Pennsylvania. Her husband, Gerald, is an insurance agent and

PLATE 114. *Brooksville Woman's Club quilt. Designed by Florence Renney and constructed in 1984 by twenty-two members of the club coordinated by Florence Renney. Dimensions, 97" × 105"; top of cotton-polyester blend fabrics; machine-pieced; hand-quilted; polyester batting; white cotton muslin backing.*

PLATE 115. *Rose Variation appliqué. Made in 1984 by Juliet Brown Blum of Sarasota, Florida (see also Plate 25). Dimensions, 83" × 93"; cotton top; appliquéd by hand; quilted by hand in crosshatch pattern; polyester batting; cotton muslin backing.*

Juliet Brown Blum.

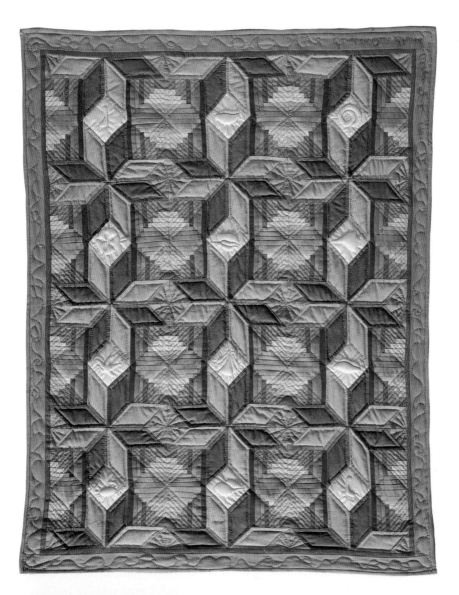

PLATE 116. *"Sand in Our Shoes." Made by Aloyse Yorko in Jupiter, Florida, in 1984. Dimensions, 34" × 44"; cotton top; pieced by hand and machine; quilted by hand in parallel pattern with wave pattern in outer border and trapunto shells and footprints; polyester batting; cotton batik backing.*

Aloyse Yorko.

they have two children. She was always interested in stitchery but was thirty-nine when she learned to quilt in an adult education class. She uses her own designs, often inspired by quilt classes, and purchases cotton fabrics especially for quilting. According to Aloyse, she quilts "all the time" in her home and uses her quilts to decorate her home. She won an award in the Mountain Mist contest in 1975 and a National Quilting Association ribbon in 1984. Aloyse was editor of *Quilt* magazine from 1979 to 1985.

An unusual family history quilt (Plate 117) was made in Pensacola, Florida, in 1985 by its owner, Parrie Ellen (Pat) Enfinger, of Pensacola. Pat was born in 1929 in Gatesville, Texas. Her wide-ranging interests include screen printing, embroidery, history, genealogy, and quilting. She is a self-taught quilter who began work in this medium at age fifty-one. Now she quilts everywhere, almost daily, and her quilts are used by friends and relatives as bedding as well as wall hangings in their homes. In making this quilt Pat used the cyanotype technique for reproducing photographs and documents that were important in her family's history, such as Civil War records and an 1841 marriage license. Pat also writes poetry, which she sometimes incorporates into her quilts.

Grace Perry Anderson is the maker and owner of a quilt she calls "Tallahassee Trees" (Plate 118). She made the quilt in 1985 at her home in Tallahassee, Florida. It is a tribute to the beautiful greenery of the state's capital city and includes meticulously pieced traditional block versions of pines, oaks, and magnolias around the Tallahassee block, which represents dogwood blossoms. The quilting is done in outlines of leaves from Grace's yard. "Tallahassee Trees" received two blue ribbons at the North Carolina Quilt Symposium in 1986.

Grace was born in 1920 in Kissimmee, Florida, and in 1945 she married Andrew Cecil Anderson, a career Army officer. As a military wife Grace has lived in twelve states, Germany, and Japan. She has always sewn clothing for herself and her family, but did not learn to quilt until she taught herself at age fifty-five. Now she quilts almost daily, primarily for her family, and has made a few commissioned quilts. Grace is also keenly interested in gardening and sports—especially those sports played by Florida State University teams.

The members of the Palm Patchers Quilt Club in Ft. Myers, Florida, made the blocks for the "City of Palms" friendship quilt (Plate 119) in 1985 and presented them to Dorothy J. Higbie, who assembled the blocks and did the quilting.

Dorothy was born in 1926 in Floral Park, New York. She and her husband, now retired, have three children. Her interests include playing bridge, sewing, cooking, and quilting. Dorothy learned to quilt at age fifty in classes and now quilts almost daily in her home. She usually uses fabrics

PLATE 117. *Family history quilt. Made by Parrie Ellen Enfinger in 1985 in Pensacola, Florida. Dimensions, 81½" × 100"; cotton top; pieced by machine; quilted by hand and machine in outline pattern; polyester batting; blue cotton backing.*

Parrie Ellen Enfinger.

PLATE 118. *"Tallahassee Trees." Made by Grace Perry Anderson in Tallahassee, Florida, in 1985. Dimensions, 70" × 70"; cotton top; pieced by machine; fine hand-quilting in echo pattern and outlines of leaves from the quilt maker's yard; polyester batting; cotton print backing.*

CITY OF PALMS

1885 1985

FORT MYERS, FLORIDA

PLATE 119. *"City of Palms." Appliquéd by members of the Palm Patchers Quilt Club, and assembled and quilted by Dorothy J. Higbie in Ft. Myers, Florida, in 1985. Dimensions,* *79½" × 81"; cotton top; pieced and appliquéd by hand; hand-quilted in outline and channel patterns with palm trees quilted in the border; polyester batting; beige cotton backing.*

purchased from quilt shops and makes quilts for decorative as well as practical purposes.

Dorothy's friends who appliquéd the blocks for the "City of Palms" quilt are as follows (blocks numbered beginning at upper left of top row). *First row*: 1 (Exhibition Hall), Toni Chartier; 2 (Bell Tower Mall), Mickie Schwam; 3 (Historical Museum [old railroad station]), Shirley Turk; 4 (Sanibel Lighthouse), Dorothy Higbie. *Second row*: 5 (Robert Stuckey Building), Lorea Zelle; 6 (McGregor Fountain), Ellen Malone; 7 (Bradford Hotel), Betty Sehorn; 8 (McGregor Boulevard), Marge Downs. *Third row*: 9 (Edison Bridge), Selma Delaney; 10 (First Federal Bank of Ft. Myers), Della Arnold; 11 (Burroughs Home), Roberta Roberts; 12 (Ft. Myers Country Club), Pauline Wetterstroem. *Fourth row*: 13 (Alliance of the Arts), Fedes Driscoll; 14 (Edison Winter Home), Kathy O'Toole; 15 (Ft. Myers High School), Lynn Lewis; 16 (Edison Congregational Church), Inge Vogler.

A lovely small wall hanging of original design, "Jeri's Flower Garden" (Plate 120), made in 1985 by its owner, Jeri Hight of Lantana, Florida, was the cover photograph for *Lady's Circle Patchwork Quilts* magazine in July 1986. Jeri was born in 1933 in Cleveland, Ohio. She is a homemaker, her husband works in aviation, and they have three children. She learned to quilt at age forty-three in Honolulu, and now works from her own original designs using scraps of satin, velvet, terry cloth, faille, broadcloth, chintz, velour, and muslin. Her quilts are used primarily for decorative purposes and she quilts almost daily at her home in Lantana.

The renewed modern interest in quilt making has made the sampler quilt popular as an introduction to quilt-making techniques and a means of learning how to make a variety of block designs. Florida Guilford, a retired teacher who lives in Tallahassee, Florida, is the owner of a pastel sampler quilt that she made in 1986 (Plate 121). Florida was born in Altha, Florida, in 1911. Before her teens Florida often helped Mrs. Turvaville, the owner of a general store in Altha, to card cotton for quilt battings. Mrs. Turvaville made quilts from the fabric swatches taken from outdated men's suit sample books in the store, and Florida observed her working on the quilts and sometimes assisted. She taught herself to quilt when her interest revived at age seventy-two. Now she quilts nearly every day, using cotton fabrics purchased for her quilting. She uses purchased templates as well as patterns from books and magazines.

Lorraine Moore of Pensacola, Florida, is the owner and maker of a contemporary quilt called "Starry Present" (Plate 122); she made the quilt in 1986 in Pensacola. Lorraine was born in 1947 in Barberton, Ohio. She is a mother, teacher, and accountant, married to a physician, and they are the parents of two children. She learned to quilt at age thirty-two, largely self-taught. She quilts at least five days a week and uses geometry and design

PLATE 120. *"Jeri's Flower Garden." Made by Jeri Hight in Lantana, Florida, in 1985. Dimensions, 37 1/2" × 48 1/2"; top of cotton, cotton-polyester blend, polyester, silk, and rayon fabrics; appliquéd by hand with hand-embroidered details; hand-quilted in parallel pattern; polyester batting; cotton muslin backing.*

PLATE 121. *Sampler quilt.*
Made in 1986 by Florida
Guilford of Tallahassee, Flor-
ida. Dimensions, 79″ × 93″;

cotton top; pieced by machine;
hand-quilted; polyester batting;
cotton backing.

PLATE 122. *"Starry Present."*
Made by Lorraine Moore in
Pensacola, Florida, in 1986.
Dimensions, 69" × 78"; cot-
ton top; pieced by hand; fine
hand-quilting in outline, inter-
locking hexagons, and stipple
patterns to form stars; polyester
batting; lavender cotton
backing.

books to develop designs and patterns. Her quilts are used by family members.

"Faceless Figures Doing Their Thing" (Plate 123) is the whimsical title given a quilt made in 1986 by Arlene Gutzeit in Gulf Breeze, Florida, and given to her husband, Karl. Arlene was born in 1916 in West Haven, Connecticut. She learned to quilt when she was nine from her grandmother. For this quilt Arlene used an original Iris Rainbow pattern published in Mary Ellen Hopkins's book *It's Okay If You Sit on My Quilt.* After her retirement from medical secretarial work, Arlene quilted almost every day at her home in Gulf Breeze and at Lake St. Peter in Ontario, Canada, until she died the year after this quilt was registered in the Florida Quilt Heritage Project.

"Piccadilly Circus" was made using the Railroad Crossing pattern by Eleanor Maloney of Atlantic Beach, Florida, in 1986 (Plate 124). Made as a sixteenth birthday present for her grandson, Richard Maloney, this quilt won best-of-show at the North Carolina Quilt Symposium in Greensboro, North Carolina, in 1987.

Eleanor was born in 1912 in Arlington, New Jersey. She received a bachelor's degree qualifying her to teach mathematics and chemistry and worked as an insurance approver and college bookstore manager. In 1937 she married William Bailey Maloney, an executive with Exxon before his retirement. While she has lived mostly in New Jersey, she also lived in London for four years and has lived in Florida since 1974. She was seventy years old before she made her first quilt in 1982 and says she has not stopped quilting since. Eleanor uses pattern and design books and magazines as sources for her designs and uses primarily fabrics purchased especially for her work. Her quilts are used on beds and as wall hangings by family members. She has submitted seven of her quilts to the National Quilting Association annual shows since 1985 and has been awarded four blue ribbons, one third-place ribbon, and one honorable mention.

The St. Lucie County historical quilt (Plate 125), owned by the St. Lucie County Historical Commission in Ft. Pierce, Florida, was made in 1986 as a group quilt by twelve individuals, all leaders in their local quilting circles. The group included several teachers of quilting and a quilt shop owner. The blocks and their creators are: Florida block, Diane B. Blair; Spanish galleon, Dora Louise Franko; brown pelican, Betty Oberg; windmill and cistern, Roberta Blank; First Baptist Church, Shirley Fallin; Florida East Coast Railroad Station, Gena Manville; St. Lucie Club, Tensie Thomas; Seminole woman, Rosalie Arnold; St. Lucie County Courthouse, Lavinia Charles; P. P. Cobb Store, Rose Sigworth; orange grove, Theresa Vachon Field; and bandstand gazebo, Grace Warren. In the block made by Rosalie Arnold, depicting a Seminole woman wearing a

PLATE 123. *"Faceless Figures Doing Their Thing." Made by Arlene Gutzeit in Gulf Breeze, Florida, in 1986. Dimensions, 40" × 87"; cotton top; hand-appliquéd; fine hand-quilting in outline, diamond grid, and floral patterns; polyester batting; white cotton-polyester blend backing.*

traditional patchwork dress, the top and left sides of the block are bordered with pieces of Seminole stripping made by an unidentified Seminole woman.

Florida's landscapes and animals seem to spring to life in the work of Audrey Finn Troutman, quilter and Audubon Society member. Her quilt "Animal Friends," an original design, was made in Vero Beach, Florida, in 1986 (Plate 126). Audrey was born in 1911 in Herndon, Pennsylvania. She is a retired teacher, wife of a salesman, and mother of one child. She learned to quilt at age sixty-three in a class at the Woman's Club in Vero Beach. Her quilts are made for both decorative and practical use and incorporate designs based on book illustrations and photographs. She also designed the Indian River County quilt that is permanently displayed at the entrance of the county commission's chambers.

The winner for the state of Florida in the Great American Quilt Contest sponsored by the American Museum of Folk Art in New York City was "Americana in Appliqué," made in 1986 by its owner, Marilyn Dorwort of Delray Beach, Florida (Plate 127). This beautifully detailed and designed quilt incorporates every appliqué technique: shadow, reverse, broderie perse, and regular appliqué. It was exhibited in New York City and throughout the United States and Japan as a part of the traveling exhibit of the Great American Quilt Contest winners. Its photograph and description are included in the book *All Flags Flying*.

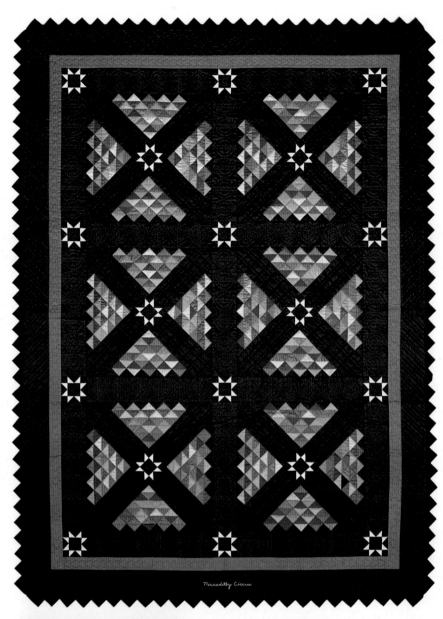

PLATE 124. *"Piccadilly Circus," made in the Railroad Crossing pattern by Eleanor Maloney of Atlantic Beach, Florida, in 1986. Dimensions, 66" × 89½"; cotton top; pieced by machine; fine hand-quilting in outline and parallel patterns; polyester batting; blue cotton backing.*

Eleanor Maloney.

PLATE 125. *St. Lucie County historical quilt. Made by twelve Ft. Pierce, Florida, quilters in 1986. Dimensions, 48″ × 63½″; top of cotton and cotton- polyester blend fabrics; pieced by hand and machine; hand- quilted; polyester batting; ivory cotton backing.*

PLATE 126. "Animal Friends." Made by Audrey Finn Troutman of Vero Beach, Florida, in 1986. Dimensions, 62" × 81"; top of cotton-polyester blend; hand-appliquéd and hand-embroidered; fine hand-quilting in outline and diamond grid patterns; polyester batting; blue cotton-polyester blend backing.

Audrey Finn Troutman.

PLATE 127. *"Americana in Appliqué." Made in 1986 by Marilyn Dorwort of Delray Beach, Florida. Dimensions, 72" × 72"; top of cotton and cotton-polyester blends; appliquéd by hand and machine; hand-quilted every ¼" diagonally through the background; polyester batting; tan cotton-polyester blend backing.*

PLATE 128. *Rose appliqué
sampler quilt. Made in 1987
in Gainesville, Florida, by the
Possum Crick Quilters. Dimensions, 83" × 102"; cotton top;
appliquéd by hand, blocks*
*assembled by machine; fine
hand-quilting in outline, diamond grid, and fan patterns;
polyester batting; cream cotton
backing.*

Marilyn was born in 1939 in Washta, Iowa. She is a quilt shop owner and is married to a retired airline pilot. She is self-taught, having learned to quilt in her late thirties. Currently she is a National Quilting Association certified teacher who teaches at her shop in Delray Beach and travels to lecture and conduct quilting workshops. Her published books include *Pines and Vines, Carousel Charmers,* and *Braid, Bows and Berries,* and she has written magazine articles for *Lady's Circle Patchwork Quilts, Patchwork Patter,* and *Needlecraft for Today.*

A Rose appliqué sampler quilt (Plate 128) was made in 1987 in Gainesville, Florida, by the Possum Crick Quilters as a raffle quilt to help defray the costs of their documentation for the Florida Quilt Heritage project. Mary Stewart of Chiefland, Florida, was the fortunate winner of the raffle. The quilt was a group project completed in work sessions in the homes of various members. They used books and magazines as sources for the rose quilt blocks.

The Possum Crick Quilters also created their own "signature" quilt, the "Possum Crick" quilt (Plate 129), made in 1987 in Gainesville, Florida. Most group members live on Possum Creek, and the quilted wall hanging includes appliquéd and embroidered representations of the native plants and animals found along the creek.

The Centennial quilt (Plate 130) owned by the Citrus County Historical Society in Inverness, Florida, was made by the Cracker Quilters in Beverly Hills, Florida in 1987 and presented by the quilters to the Citrus County Historical Society. Each appliquéd block depicts a historical event between 1887 and 1940. Those who appliquéd the blocks are as follows (blocks numbered beginning at top left corner): 1 (Houston-Ligget Cedar Mill), Helen Spivey; 2 (stagecoach), Lois Weighall; 3 (Community Church of Dunnellon), Jane Croney; 4 (fields of cattle), Lois Weighall; 5 (cotton fields), Mary Costa; 6 (log cabin), Janet Payne; 7 (cypress swamp), Lois Weighall; 8 (tortoises), Betty Hulse; 9–10 (stealing of the courthouse), Helen Spivey; 11 (cardinal), Louise Veldman; 12 (Gospel Island Bridge in Inverness), Alfreda Slavinski and Ursula Peters; 13 (fish house), Loretta Morgan; 14–20 (manatee), Helen Spivey; 17–23 (pine tree), Mary Gabig; 15–16 and 21–22 (map of Citrus County), Dorothy Miller; 18 (courthouse), Jean Innis; 19 (Yulee Sugar Mill), June Rogers; 24 (the *John L. Inglis*), June Rogers; 25 (Homasassa water tank), Dorothy Miller; 26 (pelican), Jean Innis; 27–28 (Fort Cooper "Mooning"), Mary Costa; 29 (fox squirrel), Ruth Rausch; 30 (train station at Floral City), Dorothy Sokolowski; 31 (Ozello schoolhouse), Alfreda Slavinski; 32 (Stage Stand Cemetery), Mary Costa; 33 (orange tree) and 34 ("Feeding the Nation"), Jeanette Boll; 35 (The Cracker Quilters), Ursula Peters; and 36 (Floral City Methodist

PLATE 129 (opposite). "Possum Crick." Made in 1987 by
Possum Crick Quilters of
Gainesville, Florida. Dimensions, 64" × 97"; cotton top;
appliquéd and embroidered by
hand; hand-quilted in outline
the blocks and pattern of leaves
and vines in border; polyester
batting; green cotton backing.

PLATE 130 (above). Centennial
quilt. Made by the Cracker
Quilters in Beverly Hills, Florida, in 1987. Dimensions, 83"
× 83"; cotton top; hand-appliquéd and hand-embroidered;
hand-quilted in outline and
diamond patterns; polyester batting; white cotton backing.

Church), Bessie Sanner. Georgianna Cook, Ruth Estercamp, Axie Jenkinson, and Kathryn Mulder helped with the quilting.

The Crystal River Centennial quilt (Plate 131), owned by the Citrus County Historical Society, Inverness, Florida, was made by the Creative Quilters of Citrus County in 1987 in Crystal River, Florida, and was a gift to the society from the guild. It represents a year of effort by twenty members of the Creative Quilters. Historical sites in the county were drawn from old and current photographs, designs drafted, and blocks constructed by individual members.

The quilters who created the blocks are as follows (beginning at upper left and continuing clockwise): 1 (Heritage House, the old W. H. Edwards estate), Vi Jezischek; 2 (old Bank of Crystal River), Charlotte Gore; 3 (Calvary Baptist Church), Alma Crosby; 4 (first grade school in Crystal River), Sabina Hlavati; 5 (Holder [Miller] House), Sabina Hlavati; 6 (Crystal River Depot), Alma Crosby; 7 (Heritage Square), Ruth Brown; 8 (Plantation Inn), Joanne Chance; 9 (Dixon Hotel), Shirley Henriksen; 10 (City Hall), Betty Brown; and 11 (Woman's Club), Betty Brown. The quilting was done by Pattie Williams, Judy Monteaboro, and other members of the Creative Quilters, with some of the design credit to former member Billie Gildersleeve. The quilt has been exhibited at the Citrus County Art League, Beverly Hills, Florida, and the National Quilting Association annual quilt show in Little Rock, Arkansas, in 1988.

In 1987 Jean Meadows of Sarasota, Florida, made her "Log Cabin Village" quilt (Plate 132). Jean was born in 1939 in Tampa, Florida, and is an extension home economist. Preparing and presenting a slide lecture during 1975–77 as a Bicentennial tribute on the history and care of quilts inspired Jean to try serious quilt making. She learned to quilt at age twenty-four, self-taught, and is interested in all phases—designing, constructing, teaching, and judging. She quilts at home almost daily and even more on weekends, using scraps from clothing construction and other pieces collected from family and friends as well as some purchased fabrics. She makes both bed-size quilts and wall hangings and uses a hoop as well as a frame. Many of Jean's designs are original, and she obtains others from books and magazines.

A modern charm quilt called "Kaleidoscope" (Plate 133) was made by its owner, Joan A. Hatt of Sarasota, Florida, in 1987. Each of its 1,480 triangles is from a different piece of fabric. It won a blue ribbon at the Friendship Knot Quilters show in Sarasota in April 1988. Joan was born in 1929 in Brooklyn, New York. She is a homemaker, has three children, and is married to a surgeon. She learned to quilt at age fifty-three in a quilting class and gathers fabrics from a variety of sources—friends, bazaars, and purchases. Joan now quilts almost every day in her studio.

PLATE 131. *Crystal River Centennial quilt. Made by the Creative Quilters of Citrus County in 1987 in Crystal River, Florida. Dimensions, 64" × 105"; cotton top;* *hand-appliquéd and hand-embroidered; fine hand-quilting in crosshatch, outline, parallel, and rope patterns; polyester batting; cotton muslin backing.*

PLATE 132. *"Log Cabin Village." Made in 1987 by Jean Meadows of Sarasota, Florida. Dimensions, 72" × 72"; cotton top; pieced by hand; hand-* *quilted in clamshell, channel, crosshatch, diamond, echo, floral, stipple, and diagonal patterns; cotton batting; tan cotton backing.*

PLATE 133. *"Kaleidoscope."*
Made in 1987 by Joan A. Hatt
of Sarasota, Florida. Dimen-
sions, 69½" × 86½"; cotton
top; pieced by machine; fine
hand-quilting in outline pat-
tern; polyester batting; off-white
cotton backing.

A Florida-oriented quilt named "Marine Life" (Plate 134) is owned by Dorothy J. Higbie of Ft. Myers, Florida. It was designed by Mickey Lawler of Simsbury, Connecticut, and made by Dorothy in Ft. Myers in 1987. Dorothy was born in Floral Park, New York, in 1926. Both she and her husband are now retired. She learned to quilt through classes at age fifty and quilts almost daily in her home, making quilts for practical use as well as for decorative purposes.

Painter-turned-quilter Rita Denenberg is the creator and owner of the "Osceola, Seminole Warrior" quilted wall hanging (Plate 135) which she made in 1987 in Royal Palm Beach, Florida. Rita's original design is based on a portrait by George Catlin. Strips of Seminole patchwork adorn Osceola's clothing and headdress and form the border of the quilt. It was exhibited in the American Quilters Society annual show in Paducah, Kentucky, in 1988 and appeared on the cover of the August 1989 *Patchwork Patter*, the quarterly publication of the National Quilting Association.

Rita was born in 1933 in New York City. She is a homemaker, has five children, and her husband is retired. While living in New York City, Rita was involved in oil painting, but after learning to quilt at age forty-nine she transferred her skills in composition, design, and color from oils to thread and fabric and finds quilting a satisfying medium. She now quilts several hours almost every day in her home workshop and teaches classes in special techniques at local quilt shops. In a recent international quilt contest sponsored by the American Museum of Folk Art in New York City, Rita's crib quilt, "My Tea Party," was chosen to represent the state of Florida. The quilt was exhibited at the 1989 Great American Quilt Festival and will travel throughout the United States for three years.

The broderie perse appliqué technique is used to great advantage in the quilt "Reminiscence," made in 1987 by its owner, Yolanda Tovar of Boca Raton, Florida (Plate 136). This technique involves cutting design elements from a printed fabric (usually chintz), rearranging the elements into a new design, and applying them to a background fabric by appliqué.

Yolanda was born in 1953 in Boston, Massachusetts, and learned to embroider at age seven. Part of her early life was spent in Venezuela, where she was taught in school by French nuns and had six years of instruction in embroidery. She moved to Florida in 1980, took classes in quilting, and began to perceive quilting as an art medium. Yolanda studies antique quilts for inspiration and is skilled in drawing and designing. She uses chintz and other cotton fabrics and quilts almost every day at home. She does some commisioned works and also teaches quilting classes. Since 1983 she has entered a number of her quilts in shows and has received eight blue ribbons. Photographs of her work have appeared in *Quilt Almanac*

PLATE 134. *"Marine Life."*
Made in 1987 by Dorothy J.
Higbie of Ft. Myers, Florida;
designed by Mickey Lawler of
Simsbury, Connecticut. Dimen-
sions, 39" × 48"; cotton top;
pieced, appliquéd, and em-
broidered by hand; fine
hand-quilting in outline pat-
tern; polyester batting;
yellow cotton backing.

Dorothy J. Higbie.

Rita Denenberg.

PLATE 135. *"Osceola, Seminole Warrior." Made in 1987 by Rita Denenberg of Royal Palm Beach, Florida. Dimensions: 45" × 70"; cotton top; appliquéd and pieced by hand; handquilted in channel, echo, and floral patterns; polyester batting; multicolor cotton print backing.*

PLATE 136. "Reminiscence."
Made in 1987 by Yolanda Tovar
of Boca Raton, Florida. Dimensions, 50" × 55"; cotton
top; broderie perse hand appliqué and hand embroidery; fine
hand-quilting in parallel, outline, and basketweave patterns;
cotton batting; black cotton
backing.

Yolanda Tovar.

1986; *Lady's Circle Patchwork Quilts,* July 1986; *Quilts and Country Crafts,* 1988; and the (Fort Launderdale) *Sun Sentinel* January 30, 1987. Yolanda is also active in local quilters' organizations. She has two cats and two children—a fifteen-year-old daughter who does not sew and a ten-year-old son who loves quilts.

A bold and dramatic quilt named the *"Challenger* Space Shuttle" quilt (Plate 137) was made by its owner, Robert L. Hamilton of Titusville, Florida, in 1987. Robert was born in 1937 in Phoenix, Arizona; he is a mechanical engineer and father of three children. He watched his mother and grandmother quilt throughout his childhood and learned to quilt himself when he was forty-nine years old. Robert met the *Challenger* crew when they came into the orbiter processing facility where he was working on the space shuttle, and after their tragic death he felt a strong need to create a tribute to their memory. Once he had decided that a quilt would be appropriate, he had to learn how to make one. Robert felt that if he had the skill and eye-hand coordination to land a jet fighter on an aircraft carrier, he could learn to operate a sewing machine—and he did. He designed the quilt, made his patterns from space shuttle drawings and photographs, constructed the top, did the quilting with a lap hoop, and wrote the poem that is machine-embroidered on the quilt. He sought help from local quilters when he encountered problems. Robert's quilt adapts the most modern materials and techniques to a time-honored craft and brings Florida's quilts and quilt makers from the early nineteenth century wild frontier to the wild blue yonder of space exploration.

◆   ◆   ◆

Florida's quilt makers, quilt owners, and quilt lovers will no doubt continue to place great value on quilts as beautiful and meaningful artifacts. Throughout Florida's history, quilts have been made for practical uses, as part of a handicraft tradition handed down from generation to generation, as loving gifts, as a means of contributing to a worthy cause or commemorating an important event, and as a means of personal artistic expression. Florida does not appear to have an easily identifiable tradition of quilt making over its history; rather, great diversity and vigorous creativity are apparent in the body of more than 5,000 quilts registered for the statewide project. Perhaps the only truly distinctive quilt-related handwork done in Florida is the intricate patchwork still being made, worn, and sold by the Seminole Indians.

Florida's diverse quilting heritage began with the quilts brought into the state from other parts of the country by the early settlers and includes

PLATE 137. "*Challenger Space Shuttle.*" *Top designed and made by Robert L. Hamilton of Titusville, Florida, in 1987. Dimensions, 89" × 107"; top of cotton and cotton-polyester blend fabrics; appliquéd and embroidered by machine; hand-quilted primarily in parallel lines; polyester batting; blue cotton-polyester blend backing; poem written by Robert Hamilton in tribute to the Challenger mission and crew is machine-embroidered.*

Robert L. Hamilton.

quilts made from native materials in the early years of statehood. It also includes quilts made as people and development moved southward down the peninsula—made by slave and mistress, man and woman, black and white, rich and poor. Through the difficulties of war, depression, and natural disasters and the happy times of growth and expansion, there have been ebbs and flows of quilt-making activity in the Sunshine State, culminating in the healthy environment for quilts and quilters that is being enjoyed in Florida as the decade of the 1990s begins.

Selected Bibliography

Benberry, Cuesta. "Afro-American Women and Quilts." *Uncoverings—Research Papers of the American Quilt Study Group* (1980): 64–67.

Clarke, Bea Fleming. Interview. Tallahassee, Fla., May 11, 1989.

Douglas, Marjory Stoneman. *Florida: The Long Frontier.* New York: Harper and Row, 1967.

Eppes, Susan Bradford. *Through Some Eventful Years.* Reprint, edited by Joseph D. Cushman, Jr. Floridiana Facsimile and Reprint Series. Gainesville: University of Florida Press, 1967.

Evans, Sara M. *Born for Liberty: A History of Women in America.* New York: Free Press, 1989.

Faircloth, Evelyn Johnson. Interview. Tallahassee, Fla., June 21, 1989.

Florida Department of Commerce, Division of Tourism. *Florida's History.* Brochure co-produced with the Museum of Florida History. Tallahassee.

Florida Department of State. *A Short History of Florida.* Brochure. Tallahassee.

Florida Slave Narratives. Prepared from Federal Writers Project of the Works Progress Administration for the State of Florida 1936–38. Reprint, edited by George P. Rawick. Westport, Conn.: Greenwood Publishing Company, 1972.

Fry, Gladys-Marie. *Stitched from the Soul: Slave Quilts from the Ante-Bellum South.* New York: Dutton Studio Books, 1990.

Garoutte, Sally. "Early Colonial Quilts in a Bedding Context." *Uncoverings—Research Papers of the American Quilt Study Group* (1980): 18–25.

Groene, Bertram H. *Ante-Bellum Tallahassee.* Tallahassee, Fla.: The Heritage Foundation, 1971.

Groves, Ernest R. *The American Woman.* New York: Emerson Books, 1944.

Gunn, Virginia. "Quilts—Crazy Memories." In *America's Glorious Quilts,* edited by Dennis Duke and Deborah Harding. New York: Hugh Lauter Levin Associates, 1987.

Hanna, Kathryn A. *Florida, Land of Change.* Chapel Hill: University of North Carolina Press, 1941, 1948.

Horton, Roberta. *Calico and Beyond: The Use of Patterned Fabric in Quilts.* Lafayette, Calif.: C&T Publishing Co., 1986.

Jahoda, Gloria. *Florida: A History.* New York: W. W. Norton and Company, 1984.

Keuchel, Edward. Lecture notes from "The History of Florida." Florida State University, spring semester, 1989.

Long, Ellen Call. *Florida Breezes.* 1882. Reprint, edited by Margaret S. Chapman. Floridiana Facsimile and Reprint Series. Gainesville: University of Florida Press, 1962.

McKay, D. B., ed. *Pioneer Florida.* Tampa, Fla.: Southern Publishing Company, 1959.

Morris, Allen. *The Florida Handbook, 1989–1990.* Tallahassee, Fla.: Peninsular Publishing Company, 1989.

Orlofsky, Patsy, and Myron Orlofsky. *Quilts in America.* New York: McGraw-Hill Book Company, 1974.

Ramsey, Bets. "Design Invention in Country Quilts of Tennessee and Georgia." *Uncoverings—Research Papers of the American Quilt Study Group* (1980): 48–55.

Ryan, Mary P. *Womanhood in America from Colonial Times to the Present.* New York: New Viewpoints, 1975.

Safford, Carleton L., and Robert Bishop. *America's Quilts and Coverlets.* New York: Bonanza Books, 1985.

Shofner, Jerrell H. *History of Jefferson County.* Tallahassee, Fla.: Sentry Press, 1976.

Sims, Elizabeth H. *A History of Madison County, Florida.* Madison, Fla.: Madison County Historical Society, 1986.

Tebeau, Charlton W. *A History of Florida.* Miami: University of Miami Press, 1971.

Wilder, Donna. "Quilts at an Exhibition." In *America's Glorious Quilts,* edited by Dennis Duke and Deborah Harding. New York: Hugh Lauter Levin Associates, Inc., 1987.

Woloch, Nancy. *Women and the American Experience.* New York: A. A. Knopf, 1984.

Index

◆ ◆ ◆

The following donors contributed to the Florida Quilt Heritage book project through the Museum of Florida History, Florida History Associates:

National Quilting Association
Alma Binford
Monsanto Arts
Anne Bonner
Florida Guilford
Barbara Grine
Karl Gutzeit
S. M. Burgunder
Lorraine Blackburn
Eunice Bush
Diane Blackwood
Mary Christofferson
Dorothy Clark
William Akeridge
Miriam Barbee
Parrie E. Enfinger
Lucille Lovelady
Ella Yasecko
Clifford Morrison
Betty Beck
Betsy Gann
Katherine Stanley
Edna Earle McKee
Merle Campbell
Winifred Aguillo
Elizabeth Carter
Martha Pierce
Josephine Izett
Rosa Walker
William Driscoll
Jean Stavros
M & J Properties

Carol Bouknecht
Blanche Burgher
Margaret Klasovsky
Grace Carter
Jessie Brooks
Adelaide Klein
Dorothy McKeever
Glyndol Commander
School for Inquiring Mynds
Sandra Heck
Iva Pifer
Ezella Billings
Rosalia Dante
Edna Thurman
Constance Gosselin
Florence O'Neil
Mrs. D. D. McIntyre
Bette M. Smith
Mary Endriss
Dorothy Silar
Molly Hollow
Lois Weighall
Catherine Whitaker
Maude Ridlehoover
Dixie Haywood
Eleanor Maloney
Mary L. Cannon
Seaside Piecemakers
Ponce de Leon Homemakers
Palm Patchers
Virginia Northrop
Eleanor Mitchell

Mary Pryor
Janice Moffat
Irene Malloy
Irma Pitzor
Jean DeFrancis
Coastal Quilters
Bettie Heathcock
Jean P. Johnson
E. M. Burton
Lenora Hayes
Ruth Evans
Cracker Quilters
Carol Woicinski
Gloria Thomas
Dempsey Creary
West Pasco Quilters
Doris Hamaker
Mattiewood Staffiles
Extension Homemakers
Sara Jane Spring
Ocean Waves, NQA
Embroiderers Guild
Carolyn Maruggi
Pensacola Quilters
Field Citrus
Florida Cabin Fever Quilters
Letta Schultz
M. Konopaska
Villagers
Quilters Unlimited of Tallahassee
Mary Alice Minnick